The Jarrett-Palmer Express of 1876

COAST TO COAST IN EIGHTY-THREE HOURS

J. C. Ladenheim

HERITAGE BOOKS
2008

HERITAGE BOOKS
AN IMPRINT OF HERITAGE BOOKS, INC.

Books, CDs, and more—Worldwide

For our listing of thousands of titles see our website at
www.HeritageBooks.com

Published 2008 by
HERITAGE BOOKS, INC.
Publishing Division
100 Railroad Ave. #104
Westminster, Maryland 21157

Copyright © 2008 Jules C. Ladenheim

Other books by the author:
Alien Horseman: An Italian Shavetail with Custer
Custer's Thorn: The Life of Frederick W. Benteen

Cover: The "American" 4-4-0 engine
[Pennsylvania State Archives, Pennsylvania Central R. R. Collection]

All rights reserved. No part of this book may be reproduced or transmitted in any form or by any means, electronic or mechanical, including photocopying, recording or by any information storage and retrieval system without written permission from the author, except for the inclusion of brief quotations in a review.

International Standard Book Numbers
Paperbound: 978-0-7884-4559-0
Clothbound: 978-0-7884-7332-6

DEDICATED

to the men with vision who see the American rail system for what it could be.

I hear the locomotives rustling and roaring, and the shrill steam-whistle,

I hear the echoes reverberate through the grandest scenery in the world...

Bridging the three or four thousand miles of land travel,

Tying the Eastern to the Western sea...

—Walt Whitman, in *Leaves of Grass* (Passage to India)

CONTENTS

Preface ix
Introduction 1
Thursday, June 1 27
Friday, June 2 37
Saturday, June 3 49
Sunday, June 4 65
Bibliography 81
Index 85
About the Author 91

PREFACE

THE JARRETT-PALMER EXPRESS of 1876 is said to be the most important American train journey of the nineteenth century.[1] Not only did it require enormous preparation, but it was a highly hazardous undertaking, which, against all odds, came to successful completion.

Yet, lost in the maze of industrial expansion, the fame of the Jarrett-Palmer Express quickly faded, as the event became relegated to a casual footnote in the pages of history and its principals forgotten. Perhaps, in retelling the story, we may relive an era when riding a transcontinental train was a momentous experience.

There were twenty different engines used during the trip. In a few instances, the names of the engineers or the engine numbers have been omitted, since the *New York Herald* correspondent failed to supply this information in his dispatches.[2] Similarly, the firemen, those noble wielders of the scoop, as well as the ever-important conductors and superintendents have not been identified, not to denigrate their services, but to spare the reader a congestion of names.

Establishing arrival times was a recurrent problem. Before the adoption in 1883 of Frederick Allen's standard time zones, there were no less than six clocks in the Chicago railroad station,

---

[1] [unsigned] *Trains* No. 2, December 1942, p. 10.
[2] The reader may presume that if not otherwise mentioned, the engine was the prevailing American 4-4-0 type.

each displaying a different time, a reflection of the several railroads serving the city. Moreover, latitude as well as longitude was used to determine time. For example, the time in Buffalo, New York, differed from that in New York City, although both cities today are situated in the same modern time zone. It is also somewhat difficult to reconcile the times cited in the various newspaper articles; but in this study, I have accepted the time recorded by the *New York Herald* correspondent in his dispatches, which, in turn, was obtained from the conductor's watch. For our purposes, time is what the conductor said it was. Alas, the conductor's times were subsequently revised, so that the official time table does not always coincide with the times given to the correspondent by the conductor.

I express my great thanks to J. E. Bromley and the numerous railroad libraries and museums, which have assisted this study. These include the Railway Locomotive Historical Society, Union Pacific Railroad Museum, the Oakland Museum of California, the Union Pacific Railroad Museum, the California State Railroad Museum, the Pullman Archives of the Newberry Library and above all, the Central Pacific Railroad Photographic History Museum. I am greatly indebted to the New York Public Library for the Performing Arts and to the Theater Section of the Museum of the City of New York. Joseph Piersen and Charles Stats of the Chicago and Northwestern Historical Society most generously offered their assistance. My editor, Roxanne Carlson, was especially helpful. Lastly, I wish to thank my secretary, Mrs. Jean Ganley, who relieved me of many tedious details so that I could complete this study.

INTRODUCTION

THE CENTENNIAL CELEBRATION chose The Declaration of Independence as the starting point for the Century of American Freedom.

How would the country celebrate the American Centenary? A distinguished commission duly proposed an elaborate international exposition, the first ever held in the United States. Philadelphia, the cradle of the nation, was selected to host the celebration, and invitations went out all over the world. A large railroad station was constructed in West Philadelphia to welcome the visitors who were expected to flock there in impressive numbers. Five huge pavilions were erected on a three-hundred-acre site. In them, the genius of American industry would be exhibited, along with such recent inventions as the telephone, the mimeograph machine, the recent Colt and Winchester firearms, the Otis building elevator and the gigantic Corliss steam engine, which powered the equipment in Machinery Hall. Just as impressive were the products of the American train industry, with its stunning array of engines, diners, sleeping cars and baggage cars. Emperor Dom Pedro II, of Brazil was enthralled by his visit to the railroad pavilion. Inasmuch as he was scheduled to leave by train for San Francisco, he took special interest in the Pullman accommodations and pronounced his delight.

The other cities, New York among them, were chagrined to lose the opportunity to host the Centennial Exposition. To many New Yorkers, their city was a better symbol of the Century of

Expansion. With a population of almost two million, New York was the largest city in the United States, larger than all the capitals of Europe, except London. Its fortunes were early launched by the farsighted New York legislature, which financed the Erie Canal. The canal brought to the city millions of tons of produce annually, from as far away as Michigan and Ohio, at a cost far cheaper than the goods brought by roads to Baltimore and Philadelphia.

From its humble beginnings at the southern tip of Manhattan Island, New York expanded northward, following an ancient Indian path that the Dutch called the "Brede Weg" (Broadway). For the first fifty years, most dwellings along the road were residential, but thereafter commercial ventures appeared, followed by theaters and places of amusements. New York seemed to have been endowed with an insatiable appetite for theaters. Prominent actors chose Broadway on which to anchor their careers, among them Junius Brutus Booth, Edward Forest, Tyrone Power (great-grandfather of the film actor), Fanny and Charles Temple, all of whom were household idols both in the city and, thanks to the network of road companies, throughout the country.

Prominent among the theater producers was Henry C. Jarrett and his partner Henry (Harry) Palmer. Jarrett had been born in 1827 and had early entered the world of the theater as an actor. Around 1851, he became manager of the old Barnum Museum in Baltimore, which had been converted into a theater. From there, he gravitated to New York and joined forces in 1864 with Pennsylvania-born Palmer. Jarrett was the moving force, Palmer the accessory.

In 1866, their fortunes took an unexpected turn. The two had just returned from Europe with a production called *La Biche au Bois* (the Doe in the Woods) featuring ballet dancers from Paris,

London and Berlin. They planned to open the production at the Academy of Music at 14th Street and Irving Place. Before the ballet could be staged, the theater burned down, leaving the two producers with a troop of idle dancers and 110 tons of costumes and scenery. Undaunted, Jarrett proclaimed his faith in his troop, insisting that "[women's] legs are staple articles and will never get out of fashion while the world lasts."

Jarrett searched for another theater and cast his eyes on the Niblo Gardens on the northeast corner of Broadway, between Houston and Price Streets. The Niblo had been around since 1830. Earlier, it had been a restaurant and garden but was later converted into a fully equipped theater with 3,500 seats. He approached the manager and quickly entered into an agreement to incorporate his ballet production into a second rate melodrama, called *The Black Crook*, which was about to open at the Niblo. Mingling dancers and drama had never been done before on Broadway.

Jarrett completely revamped the stage play, turning it into a spectacular musical production, with fairyland motif and a huge ballet of 100 shapely chorines in pink tights. It became the most costly, daring and ornate show ever staged.

The plot by author Charles M. Barras was banal, even by the standards of the mid-nineteenth century. A hodge-podge of *Faust* and Carl Maria von Weber's *Der Freischuetz*, the plot may be quickly summarized, if only to show its absurdity. The wicked hunchback, the Black Crook, has made a contract with the Devil to deliver him one soul in return for an extra year of life. Rudolph, a painter in love with his beloved Amena, has been imprisoned in the castle dungeon of Count Wolfenstein, who himself is in love with Amena. The Black Crook pretends to arrange for Rudolph's escape, promising to lead him to a crock of gold, but instead, plans to deliver him to the Devil. On the way to his doom, the hero saves the life of a dove, which is transformed into the Queen of the Golden Realm. She takes the hero to fairyland, rescues him from the wicked Count and helps him win the hand of his beloved, while the Black Crook is dragged off to the underworld. Initially, the playwright expressed a reluctance to allow the estimable quality of the script to be compromised, but was won over with the payment of $1,500.

Jarrett and Palmer sank $55,000 into the production, the most expensive theater investment ever made. Extensive alterations to the theater were required. The ground under the theater was excavated and traps built into the stage floor so that the scenery could descend immediately with the scene changes. Scenery rose from the floor; fairies, suspended by invisible wires, flew with abandon through the air; crystal grottos dazzled the eye; babbling fountains and flashes of lightning enthralled the audience; all under the watchful direction of 114 stagehands. Nothing like this had ever before been seen on Broadway. Into an age of the flat backdrop, *The Black Crook* introduced new concepts of dynamic architectural design and vibrant scene transformations. The four-act extravaganza lasted five and three-quarters hours (7:15 P.M. to 1:00 A.M.), with the audience completely enthralled.

Success was immediate and exceeded even the most extravagant expectations. Until then, the Can-Can had been slowly gaining notoriety, and the news of French ballet dancers on Broadway immediately evoked interest, even if, as it turned out, the Can-Can was not performed. The *danseuse's* split, however, was performed for the first time. The girls were clad in flesh-colored tights, with exposed legs, in an age when the display of ankles was considered immodest. At opening night,

Introduction

September 12, 1866, the first playgoer, a woman, was refused admission, not for reasons of modesty, as was generally supposed, but in deference to an old theater superstition that bars a woman as the first admission. Although the ban was promptly rescinded, it caused a sensation and whetted the public appetite. Respectable women attended the performance, but many chose to wear veils. Prominent clergymen railed against the play, and the condemnation of the *New York Herald*, ensured an overflow attendance:

> Let all husbands and parents and guardians who value the morals of their wives, their daughters and their wards bear a watch full eye on their charges and keep them out of the walls of Niblo's Garden during the reign of the Black Crook. If any of the Herald's readers in spite of its warning and advice are determined to gaze on the indecent and dazzling brilliancy of the Black Crook, they should provide themselves with a piece of smoked glasses.

Quite likely, James Gordon Bennett, Jr., the publisher of the *Herald*, framed this blue-nosed critique tongue-in-cheek, in order to encourage attendance, since he owed a debt of gratitude for another matter to the theater manager.

The Black Crook was the most successful production ever to reach Broadway. Among the songs it helped popularize, were "The Amazons' March," "The Broadway Opera," "The Bowery Crawl," and the provocative "You Naughty, Naughty men!" sung with the *chanteuse* downstage facing the audience. Songs were revised from time to time, and new ones substituted. The play ran for an astonishing (for then) 474 performances over sixteen months and returned in succeeding years for further runs.

Henry Jarrett, Impresario.
[Billy Rose Theatre Collection, New York Public Library for the Performing Arts, Astor, Lenox and Tilden Foundation.]

Introduction 7

All society attended the show, including Charles Dickens, Woodrow Wilson, Walt Whitman and Buffalo Bill Cody (who was taken to the Niblo Theater by James Gordon Bennett). Wrote Mark Twain, the special correspondent of the *Alta California*, who saw the show at least twice:

> Beautiful bare-legged girls hanging in flower baskets; others stretched in groups on great sea shells; others clustered around fluted columns; others in all possible attitudes; girls—nothing but a wilderness of girls—stacked up, pile on pile, away aloft to the dome of the theatre.

It is said that the initial production grossed one million dollars, not including the proceeds from the road companies which took the play to Britain for 204 performances and over the entire United States to more than twenty cities. According to the playwright, the only city not visited was Sitka, Alaska. Eight times the show returned to Broadway for successful revivals, with vaudeville dancing eventually replacing the original ballet. A silent film was made in 1916, and the stage production was revived in Hoboken, New Jersey, as late as 1929, with the ballet choreographed by Agnes De Mille, in her first big success. Vestiges of the musical appeared in Sigmund Romberg's *Girl in Pink Tights* and in Twentieth Century Fox's musical *Gone are the Days*, with Monte Woolley. The play was considered by many to be the precursor of the American musical comedy, but others point out that since the music was composed by a multitude of composers, the play should more properly be regarded as a forerunner of the burlesque tradition.

Jarrett and Palmer were thereafter recognized as Broadway's leading impresarios. They continued to enjoy great prosperity with other productions in Boston, Philadelphia, Washington and

Baltimore. When Edwin Booth lost his lease, they rented the Booth Theater, and in 1876 they had a successful run with *Julius Caesar* and then with *Henry V*, starring the well-known actor Lawrence Barrett. Plans were made at the conclusion of the *Henry V* run to take the play to San Francisco, where the production was scheduled to open on Monday, June 5.

At this point, the fertile mind of Jarrett cast about for a way to exploit the situation. In order for the actors to appear in San Francisco for the scheduled opening, they would have to leave New York at least ten days before. How could Jarrett prolong the successful run on Broadway and still be in San Francisco on time? No producer likes to close a run while it is still drawing a full house. He pondered a way to use the excitement generated by the Centenary to promote his production. Jarrett carefully studied the cards he held in his hand: the play, the scheduled railroad trip to San Francisco, and the Centenary. The idea came to him of an express, cross-country railroad trip as an adjunct to the Centenary celebration.

Railroads were the pride and passion of the American public, the keystone of an expanding industrial revolution. A primitive engine, built by Oliver Evans, crept along the streets of Philadelphia as early as 1804. Initially, engines moved on a hard roadbed, while horse-drawn coaches ran on wooden tracks. In 1824 or thereabouts, John Stevens put the steam engine onto tracks, presaging the age of the railroad. In brisk succession, the Charleston-Hamburg line appeared in 1827; the Mohawk and Hudson between Albany and Schenectady in 1831; in addition to many short lines built to service quarries and mines. Railroad growth, thereafter, was exponential. Already by 1837 many hundreds of miles of rail line had been laid. Before the Civil War, there were four different gauges (track widths), but thereafter the gauge was standardized at four feet, eight and one half inches (the Roman gauge), although narrow gauges were sometimes used for short hauls or for reasons of economy.

The Civil War gave great impetus to railroad activity. It was perhaps the first major conflict in which the railroad was employed as a primary instrument of logistics. Not long after the war, the United States had as much rail track as the whole of Europe. In 1862, President Abraham Lincoln authorized an American transcontinental railroad, but no appreciable work was begun until after the cessation of hostilities, when the Central Pacific began building eastward and the Union Pacific in the opposite direction.

Work by both companies continued for six years with ever increasing vigor: three strokes to a spike, ten spikes to a rail, four hundred rails to the mile, and 1,800 miles to be spanned. Thirty vessels sailed from New York via Cape Horn to San Francisco, transporting iron, locomotives, rails and rolling stock for the Central Pacific. The materiel for the Union Pacific came by boat and wagon by way of Chicago and St. Louis. Early hopes that this transcontinental rail line would serve as a shortcut to the Orient for European goods were dispelled in 1869 by the opening of the Suez Canal, although the Panama Railroad, built in 1853, had already connected the Atlantic with the Pacific.

The junction of the two rail systems came on May 10, 1869, at Promontory Point, Utah, whereupon the transcontinental journey was reduced from five months to ten days. Five days after the union, regular transcontinental train service was begun.

Both railroads hastened to improve their highly provisional systems. They straightened road beds, smoothed grades and reconstructed bridges, tunnels, trestles and culverts. For hundreds of miles, the Union Pacific had used cottonwood, treated with zinc chloride, in the vain hope of prolonging durability. For the steeper grades, both companies laid ordinary track, weighing fifty pounds per linear yard, fully aware that heavier track was required. In many places, the roadbed had been built no wider than the width of the tie, instead of the mandated fourteen feet. The accepted practice of the day was to complete a line in the shortest time, then to improve it with operating revenue.

Transcontinental traffic began with two classes of accommodation. The emigrants paid forty dollars (or thereabouts) for passage from Omaha to San Francisco and were furnished with a narrow, wooden seat. They took their meals from station purveyors during the brief train stops. Occasionally a sandwich vendor or "butcher boy" would pass down the aisle with a tray of wares. Too often the emigrant car was shunted to the side to make way for the express trains, where they could remain for a day or more in blazing heat or freezing cold. First class passengers paid $80 to $150 and rode in beautiful wooden cars with plush velvet seats that could be pushed back to a resting position. The first class cars had steam heat and fresh linen, and their passengers took their meals at train stops in the primitive station restaurants. Later, Pullman and Wagner introduced their elegant "hotel" cars, which set the standard for first class travel.

Jarrett searched for some means of using the forthcoming railroad trip to publicize his new production of *Henry V*, scheduled to open June 5 in San Francisco. What if a spectacular transcontinental express trip could be arranged which would break all existing speed records? Suppose the allotted time could be cut in half—or less? Heretofore, the transcontinental trip was advertised to take ten days, but more often additional time was required because of breakdowns, washouts, faulty repairs or blizzards.

Many problems would have to be resolved. Would the railroad companies sanction such a trip? Could they be persuaded to act in concert? What kind of rolling stock would be used? It would be desirable from the passenger standpoint if the same passenger car could be used throughout the entire trip, although this was not the current practice. Who would pay for the trip? Our crafty producers would prefer, of course, in the grand tradition of the theater, that it be financed with other people's money.

The financing proved to be the easiest difficulty to surmount. Jarrett was able to interest James Gordon Bennett, Jr., the publisher of the *New York Herald,* in the venture. Bennett had inherited the newspaper from his father and had thrown his energies into its management. He belonged to a new generation of publishers which was as comfortable with creating news as it was in reporting it. It was Bennett who sent Stanley in 1871 to find Dr. David Livingstone in central Africa. Many other examples of his initiative would be forthcoming in later years.

When the project was explained to him, Bennett immediately saw its potential. He agreed to pay half the expenses, provided that the *Herald* (and the Associated Press) would be given exclusive rights to the newspaper story; and that the *Herald* could transport its newspapers on the train. Bennett eased the way for Jarrett to approach Horace Porter, the vice president of the Pullman Company, then residing in New York, who was in charge of Pullman's eastern and European operations. Porter, a West Point graduate, had served during the Battle of Chickamauga and later as a staff officer to General Ulysses Grant. He joined the Pullman Company in 1873 as an executive assistant to George Pullman, the founder and president of the company.

Porter, too, was delighted with the project. He insisted as a requirement for his company's participation, that the Pullman cars be used exclusively for the entire trip. Hitherto, it was the practice for the Pacific Central Railroad to substitute their own preference in sleeping cars (usually a Wagner Hotel Car), once the train left Ogden, Utah. Porter put Jarrett in touch with the five railroads which owned track between New York and San Francisco.

Mr. Thomas A. Scott, president of the Pennsylvania Railroad and a protege of General Herman Haupt, the Civil War railroad czar, was especially enthusiastic. He owed his position as president of the Pennsylvania in part to the influence of George Pullman, who also had installed him on the Pullman board of directors. Since the Pennsylvania Railroad would be carrying the major load of passengers for the Centenary, it could only benefit from the extra publicity occasioned by the transcontinental trip. The Pennsylvania Railroad boldly proposed to make its run from New York to Pittsburgh using only one engine, to demonstrate the merits of its powerful locomotive. Not to be outdone, the Central Pacific made a matching offer for its own prize engine on the vastly more difficult run from Ogden to San Francisco.

Jarrett stressed the urgency of speed, letting it be known, whether true or not, that he would suffer ruinous penalties and forfeitures if he did not open his play on Monday, June 5, in San Francisco. In a surprisingly short time, an agreement was reached among the five railroad companies. Whatever obstacles that remained were swept aside amid the exuberance engendered by the national Centennial celebration.

Newspapers carried an advertisement soliciting passengers willing to pay five hundred dollars for the privilege of a seat on the historic transcontinental journey. The fare would include a week's stay at the newly-opened Grand Palace Hotel in San Francisco and a return trip on a regular train, to be concluded within six months. Passengers would be spared the need for annoying transfers but would remain on the same train for the entire trip.

Unparalleled Run
Across the Continent
JARRETT & PALMER'S
Special Fast Trans-Continental Train
New York to San Francisco

Leaving New York on Thursday, June 1, arriving at San Francisco on Sunday June 4.
Having the Right of Way across the Continent Carrying the United States Mail, Wells Fargo & Co's Express
And Thursday's Edition of the New York Herald

Actually, five hundred dollars was not an exorbitant price, since it included a return trip and a week's stay at a world-class hotel. The cost of a first class return ticket to San Francisco at that time could be as much as three hundred dollars, without the added expense of a stopover in San Francisco. The Pullman sleeping arrangements cost an additional fifty dollars or more each way. Meals were paid for by the passenger.

Jarrett had tickets made expressly for the occasion. Ten tickets, engraved on special plates, were bound in a four by five-inch booklet, with a solid silver outer cover. The book was packaged in a white case lined with satin. The cost of tickets and case was forty dollars. The conductors were instructed to punch, but not detach, the tickets, so that they could be retained as souvenirs.

Forty passengers could be accommodated, but, as it turned out, only eighteen or so traveled the entire distance to the Pacific, the others debarking along the way. Railroad officials boarded and left the train en route. Among the passengers were C. F. Williams, the correspondent for the *New York Herald;* Henry Caril of the *Journal de Debats* (Paris); Milton Prior of the *Illustrated London News*; "Bull Run" Russell of the *London Times*, as well as two British army officers. Private citizens included P. Rawson, Alfred and Hyatt Morrison, T. Dougherty, Alfred Monere, Meyer Silverstine, Hon. Thomas J. Creamer and Dr. A. Arndt of New York; E. N. Parker and F. W. Eldridge of Chicago; C. A. Weid of Connecticut and Warren Emerson of Boston.

The five railroad companies drew up detailed plans to ensure that coal, water, food and locomotives would be available. Six thousand dispatchers, signalmen, trainmasters, division superintendents, station masters and maintenance men all received painstaking instructions to ensure that the train would have a clear and fast track. Railroad personnel were tirelessly rehearsed to ensure that the train had a rapid fueling and watering. The Union Pacific sent out orders to construct ramps and platforms on both sides of certain operating stops to facilitate the delivery of coal and water. Laborers were drilled to run up the ramps with basketfuls of coal and buckets of water, rather than hand them up one by one. The railroad still maintained tight discipline in the grand Civil War tradition of General Herman Haupt. On one occasion, Colonel Thomas A. Scott, now president of the Pennsylvania Railroad, moved Hooker's army of thirteen thousand Union troops from Virginia to Chattanooga over tracks of differing gauges in seven days, without a hitch! For these railroad companies, accustomed to move armies, a transcontinental journey was a manageable challenge.

Obviously, the regulation speeds of forty miles per hour on eastern tracks and twenty-two miles per hour on western tracks would no longer be followed. Henceforth, the watchword would be "as fast as possible." Five scheduled stops were planned, corresponding to the change of carriers. The parties concluded that if a mean speed of around forty miles per hour could be maintained, the crossing could be made in eighty-four hours. This would allow actors and producers to arrive in time for the planned opening of *Henry V* in San Francisco on June 5 (Monday). Accordingly, Jarrett made arrangements for a sumptuous banquet to be served the passengers upon their arrival Sunday, June 4.

As the day of departure approached, Jarrett and Palmer might have begun to be concerned that the public was not quite as embroiled in the excitement, as the event deserved. Some newspapers were reluctant to report the trip in detail, since Bennett (and the Associated Press) had been given exclusive rights to the reportage. For this reason, perhaps, the sale of tickets may not have been as brisk as the partners would have desired.

Arrangements had been made with the post office to carry express mail to Pittsburgh, Chicago, Omaha, Sacramento and San Francisco. No fewer than 40,000 letters were received for express delivery en route. Each letter was given a special franking imprint: *"Jarrett and Palmer Special Fast Transcontinental Run."* The letters were then sorted by destination and bagged in gaily colored mail sacks, each with a different color, corresponding to the scheduled stop. Also, an agreement was made with Wells Fargo for the express transport of packages. On Wednesday, May 31, the U.S. Mail sacks were loaded onto a Dodd's Express wagon, lavishly decorated with flags and colored lamps and drawn by six magnificent gray horses. Holding the reins was the company's chief driver and beside him, the president of the company. The mail was rushed at a gallop to the Courtland Street ferry landing for delivery across the Hudson River to the waiting train in Jersey City. Trains did not enter New York from the south until 1910, when a tunnel was constructed for the Pennsylvania Railroad.

As the curtain rang down Wednesday night, May 31, on their final performance of *Henry V*, the actors and production staff were taken to the Astor Hotel for the traditional farewell dinner of *fois gras* and champagne. Failure to do this would have flaunted a hallowed theater tradition, which Jarrett and Palmer could ill ignore, since before them lay the prospect of a rather perilous rail journey. After the meal, the three actors, Lawrence Barrett, Fred Thorpe and C. P. Bishop, together with the two producers, were rushed by cab to the Courtland Street ferry landing. There, they were joined by the passengers who had been transported to the ferry landing from their gathering place at the *Herald* office on Broadway and Anne Street. Palmer fretted that he had left behind at the Booth Theater the posters for the new production. As the party boarded the ferry boat, they were treated to a lively band concert and fireworks display, provided by Messrs. Jarrett and Palmer. The party crossed the river to the railroad yard in Jersey City, where their train awaited them.

Jersey City Railroad Terminal.
[Pennsylvania State Archives, Pennsylvania Central R. R. Collection.]

For the journey from New York to Pittsburgh, the carrier would be the Pennsylvania Railroad Company. The Pennsylvania had been organized in 1846 by concerned business leaders of Philadelphia, who were disturbed by the high cost of transporting freight across the Appalachians. New York had the Erie Canal; Baltimore, the National Road, but to reach Philadelphia in the early days, produce from trans-Appalachia could be more cheaply shipped down the Ohio and Mississippi rivers by boat to New Orleans and thence to Philadelphia by ship.

The Pennsylvania Railroad was started as a short line[3] chartered by the Commonwealth of Pennsylvania and slowly grew by absorbing other trunks. With the acquisition of the United New Jersey Railroad and Canal Company, the Pennsylvania reached

---

[3] Pennsylvania Central.

Jersey City, across the river from New York. In western Pennsylvania, the Appalachian Mountains were considered an insurmountable obstacle until the completion in 1854 of the famous horseshoe curve outside of Altoona, opening the way to the west. From the very start, the Pennsylvania Railroad was grounded in the public interest and enjoyed a widely respected reputation for punctuality. Its management was attentive to new ideas and prided itself on avoiding the financial buccaneering that had plagued the New York Central at the hands of "Commodore" Cornelius Vanderbilt, to the detriment of its stockholders; (although the Pennsy's president, Thomas Scott, had been accused of shifty dealings with the Texas railroads). Until its tragic demise in 1970, the Pennsylvania had never missed payment of a dividend check to its stockholders.

The Pennsylvania Railroad was delighted to have an opportunity to display its wares to the public, since it was expected to carry the lion's share of passengers traveling to the Centennial Celebration in Philadelphia. It was the only road in the world that could make its assigned run without stopping to take on water. This they were able to do because track pans (water troughs) had been laid between the tracks, which could be scooped up while the train was in motion. Notwithstanding, a reserve supply of water was carried in the baggage car. The Pennsylvania had macadam rail beds, block signals, a few steel cars, but still used link and pin coupling. Steel rails were scheduled to supplant the iron rails by the following year.

Above all, the Pennsylvania was the earliest railroad to employ the Westinghouse braking system, which the engineer operated. Air brakes had first been installed by the Pennsylvania in 1869 and made standard in 1870. Prior to this, cars had been equipped with a hand brake or with the chain brake. The chain brake had a wound spring attached to the brake staff. When the engineer pulled a cord, the coil springs were released from the brake shoes, allowing the brake to press against the wheel. The Westinghouse system used compressed air for braking. In the newer version, compressed air and an auxiliary air reservoir continuously pressed in equilibrium against the brake cylinder. To stop the train, the engineer released compressed air though the escape valves, upsetting the equilibrium. This caused the pressure remaining in the reservoir to press against the brake piston.

Even with all the safety devices, train travel carried a risk, albeit lessened by the relatively slow speeds of the American rail systems. Speeds of seventy-eight miles per hour had been achieved in Great Britain, where the rail beds were relatively straight, but in the United States where the rail bed generally conformed to the typography, travel was slower, (although a speed of seventy-nine miles per hour had been reported on an eighty-one-mile stretch from Syracuse to Rochester). In the early days of the railroad, rail travel was sixty times *less* dangerous than stage coach. In 1829 a coach traveler counted nine turnovers in the trip from New York to Cincinnati; but by the 1850's the halcyon days of safe railroad travel were ended, as the speed increased.

The "American" 4-4-0 engine.
[Pennsylvania State Archives, Pennsylvania Central R. R. Collection.]

Drawn up at the station awaiting its passengers, the Jarrett-Palmer Express consisted of an engine-tender, a commissary car and the Pullman Palace Hotel Car.[4] A huge crowd of well-wishers were on hand for the departure. Heaps of fresh flowers bedecked the platform. Watchmen patrolled the station to guard the train from sabotage.

The engine was the thirty-six-ton *#573*, the *Governor Tilden*, Pennsylvania's swiftest locomotive, also known as the "American Class D type." It was the prevailing 4-4-0 with four

---

[4] The *New York Herald* on May 31, 1876 describes the train as consisting of the baggage car, the Hotel Car (*Thomas A. Scott*); and the sleeping car *(Yosemite)*. On June 1, the day of departure, Mr. C. F. Williams, the *New York Herald* correspondent who accompanied the train, describes it as consisting of baggage car, Commissary Car *#202*; and Palace Hotel Car *Marlborough #311*. I have accepted the June 1 description of C. F. Williams.

pilot wheels, four driver wheels and no tracker wheels. The four pilot wheels (two on each side) helped the engine negotiate the curves. Behind them, four large driver wheels (two on each side) supported the weight of the engine, gave the locomotive great adhesion to the rails and provided the main driving force. The *#573's* four driver wheels measured five feet, ten inches in diameter and had a connection bar. The drivers were oiled through copper pipes. At a later time, small tracker wheels would be placed under the firebox, to support the growing size of the boilers.

The *#573* (David Kerr, engineer) had been built in 1872 in the Altoona shop. It generated a steam pressure of 125 pounds, had a twenty-four-inch piston stroke and was fitted with a Westinghouse braking system. The engine bore no ornamental brass except for the engine number.

The tender had a 2,400-gallon capacity. It carried 136 bushels of coal, judged sufficient to take the train to Pittsburgh without refueling, but, as a precaution, it brought extra bushels of coal in the baggage car. The management was insistent on making the run to Pittsburgh without a single operating stop.

Behind the engine-tender stood the red baggage car, with the words *"Pennsylvania"* and *"Jarrett and Palmer"* inscribed in gold leaf above the windows on each side of the car. The baggage car held a reserve wooden tank holding 2,000 gallons of water. A small donkey engine stood ready to pump the water into the tender, if required. The baggage car also carried 3,000 pounds of coal, which could be shoveled through the end door into the top of the tender. "Baggage smashers" handed up the passengers' trunks, which contained their wardrobes for San Francisco. A small printing press was set up inside the baggage car, so that news bulletins could be distributed at the stops along the way. A rack of shotguns was brought along, and scenery and costumes carefully stowed. Fifteen thousand copies of the *New York Herald* were also loaded aboard. They had been printed on Wednesday, May 31, but were postdated June 1 and were delivered in large bundles to the baggage car, where the baggage men folded and bagged them, while the train was underway.

Next came the *#202,* a twelve-wheeler commissary-smoking car, called a "combine," being a combination of coach and baggage car. Like the baggage car, it was painted red, with the words *"Pennsylvania"* and *"Jarrett and Palmer"* inscribed on each side. Food and supplies were carried in this car, and it was used by the trainmen for their repose, when off duty. There were no friction plates between the cars, so the trainmen could not escape the treacherous jolts and jerks when passing from one car to another.

Lastly, was the thirty-ton Pullman Palace Hotel Wagon, called the *Marlborough #311,* in which the passengers rode and slept. The car had been brought up from Philadelphia, where it had been on display at the Exposition. It was marked with the same inscriptions as the other cars, had steel springs and was mounted on twelve wheels. The interior was elegantly upholstered and trimmed with black walnut and silver.

The *Marlborough* was divided into three sections. The forward part contained the dining area, in which as many as five tables were positioned on both side of the compact kitchen, each accommodating four passengers. The tables were portable and, when not in use, could be stowed out of sight. Beneath the kitchen floor was a trap door, leading to the ice boxes and provisions. The special dining car did not begin long distance service until the following year.

Interior Pullman Palace Car.
[Pennsylvania State Archives, Pennsylvania Central R. R. Collection.]

A brief selection from a typical menu might include the following items:

BROILED

Porterhouse Steak	.75	Spring Chicken	1.00
with mushrooms	1.00	Bacon	.40
Mutton-Chops	.50	Boiled Ham	.40
with tomato sauce	.75	Lamb Chops	.50
Veal Cutlets, breaded	.50		

et cetera

COLD DISHES

Boiled Tongue	.40	Pickled Lobster	.40
Boiled Ham	.40	Spiced Oysters	.40
Raw Oysters	.50		

et cetera

Breakfast Wines—Claret and Sauterne
Champagne Wines—Heidsick and Krug

To the rear of the dining section, was the dormitory sleeping area for the conductor, steward and his assistants, and their toilets. Black waiters and compartment attendants, faultlessly attired in white, served the needs of the passengers. The attendants set up writing or gaming tables, pressed clothing, and prepared the sleeping accommodations. The suggested tip for the attendant was twenty-five cents per attendant per day.

Behind the forward area was the seating section for the passengers. On both sides of the aisle were fifteen rows of upholstered sofas, each two rows facing each other. As many as thirty-

Introduction 25

six to forty passengers ordinarily could be accommodated, but the Express had half that number. The section was adorned with plush carpets, mirrors and carved woodwork. Spitoons were liberally distributed. Toward dusk, the sleeping car attendants converted each set of facing sofas into five sleeping berths, with clean bedding, thick hair mattresses and double blankets for the cold nights. Ventilation was provided through the roof vents, and windows could be raised up to fifteen inches.

In the third section were dressing ("saloon") and toilet areas for both sexes. The toilet had a dry hopper with a wood seat and a tin urinal. Wastes dropped directly onto the track. A small tin water dispenser was set up outside the "saloon," and a tin cup on a chain provided for passenger use. There was also a small rear platform from which the passengers could survey the scenery.

The Pullman Hotel Cars were wider than the usual passenger car and higher as well, since the upper berth had to be hinged up to the ceiling. The extra height and width initially prevented the cars from negotiating tunnels and narrow bridges, but eventually both those structures were modified to conform to the requirements of these highly popular cars. Some national railroads used the Wagner Hotel Cars, but the Pullman was thought by most to have outshone the competition.

THURSDAY, JUNE 1

AT 12:40 A.M., Mr. Jarrett raised his arm in a theatrical signal, and the engineer sounded the steam whistle. To the cry of "Clear the Train!" the passengers quickly boarded and took their seats. Hearty "Goodbyes!" and "God Speed!" were heard. The band on the platform struck up a tune and the spectators cheered. There followed a delay as the final copies of the *Herald* were loaded, but at 1:00 A.M. the Jarrett-Palmer Express finally departed, amid the thunderous cheers of the spectators. As the train pulled away, one of the spectators threw a shoe after it. Long lines of trackmen lined the track, each holding a lantern. Aboard the train were six officers of the Pennsylvania Railroad, who would leave at Pittsburgh; two passengers who would depart in Chicago and two train linemen whose instruments might be required in the event of an accident.

The conductor began his rounds by punching the tickets. He was usually an authoritative personality, into whose hands was entrusted the welfare of the train. Trainmen and passengers disregarded his instructions at their peril. If a railroad supervisor was traveling on the train, the supervisor *conferred* with, rather than ordered, the conductor. Most passengers carried with them a guidebook, which they consulted as the train approached an interesting destination. The books informed the passengers that on the Palace Hotel Car they need not wear the white linen dusters required on the ordinary transcontinental passenger cars.

The train passed through a darkened Newark, New Jersey. Large bonfires were lit in Elizabeth. At Linden, a band was on hand, but the passengers heard only a passing note. At Rahway and Union, cannons were fired, but the passengers saw only the muzzle flash. As the train passed each depot, the railway workers lined the platform, holding lanterns. By the time Brunswick, New Jersey, was reached, the engineer had regained the time lost in Jersey City and had even run a stretch of six miles in seven minutes.

West Philadelphia, Pennsylvania, was reached at 2:31 A.M., one minute ahead of schedule. Engineer Andrew Chambers climbed aboard in relief. The ninety miles from Jersey City had been spanned in ninety-one minutes!

The West Philadelphia station was a marvel, costing $240,000, the most expensive of those built by the Pennsylvania Railroad. It fronted 120 feet of Market Street and had eight platform tracks. Bundles of *Herald* newspapers were thrown from the baggage car, as the train whizzed by the station.

The Centenary grounds in the Fairmont Park area loomed ahead. In tribute to the Jarrett-Palmer Express, lights still illuminated the buildings and grounds. By now, most passengers had retired, but Jarrett, Barrett and the Pennsylvania officials surveyed the fairyland spectacle from the rear platform of the car. Preparation of the sleeping berths had been delayed because of the late departure. Porters reported difficulty in laying out the bedding, since at high speeds they needed both hands to hold onto the berth. Because of the summer heat, windows had to be opened. Cinders from the engine smokestack soon begrimed the faces of the sleeping passengers.

Eagle, Pennsylvania, was passed at 2:58 A.M., one-half minute ahead of schedule, but thereafter the many curves in the track caused slowing. They arrived at Harrisburg at 5:19 A.M., where

Engineer Sol Hoffmaster relieved Mr. Chambers. Three thousand people thronged the platform, cheering the train. As it pulled out of the depot, copies of the *Baltimore Sun* were pitched into the baggage car for the passengers' intelligence.

Thereafter, the train began the slow ascent of the Alleghenies, eventually meeting a grade of ninety-six feet to the mile. At the time, a two percent gradient was considered to be the limit of incline (although the Baltimore & Ohio elsewhere had constructed a grade of 2.2%). Unfortunate for the Pennsylvania Railroad, their route to Chicago lay over a mountain chain, while the competition, the New York Central, had a water-level route along the Great Lakes. Since the *#573* had a light consist (i.e., it had only three cars), it rejected the services of a helper engine.

The sun rose clear and warm. When the train reached Altoona, William Philips scrambled up into the cab as relief engineer. Seated at the breakfast table, the passengers waved to the large throng standing on the platform, who watched them speed by. The Pennsylvania Railroad operated its own locomotive foundries in Altoona, unlike the other railroad companies which relied on independent shops. The historic Horseshoe Bend was reached at 8:33 A.M., a sight to behold, even today. The length of the switchback is 2,375 feet, with the west side 1,322 feet higher than the east. It had been the final obstacle to surmounting the Alleghenies. The difficulties were finally overcome in 1854, reducing railroad travel from Philadelphia to Pittsburgh from three and one-half days to less than thirteen hours. After reaching the summit, the train began its descent, traveling through two historic tunnels, the larger measuring 3,612 feet. The guidebooks informed the traveler that henceforth all rivers and streams would drain into the Mississippi or the Gulf of Mexico, until the Rockies were reached.

With every sharp curve, glasses went rattling to the floor. Because of the swaying cars, the preparation and service of hot meals presented difficulties. In the days ahead, the passengers sometimes would have to content themselves with cold chicken and a bottle of beer.

As the train neared Pittsburgh, the passengers began to see innumerable chimneys and foundries. Factory smoke soon obscured the sunlight. Pittsburgh was reached at 10:42 A.M., two minutes ahead of schedule. The 444-mile run from Jersey City to Pittsburgh had been made without a single stop, with an average speed of forty-five miles per hour. They were now **ten hours and five minutes** out of New York.

At Pittsburgh, the *Herald* correspondent rushed his dispatch to the telegraph office. Henceforth, his articles would be posted outside the newspaper offices throughout the country, where enthusiastic crowds would eagerly follow the progress. In Pittsburgh, Henry Palmer left the train for some unknown reason, as did the six officers of the Pennsylvania Central Railroad. Telegrams were delivered to the passengers, and mail pouches and bundles of the *New York Herald* were off-loaded. "Here's your *New York Herald*, this morning's edition!" screamed the newsboys on the platform, provoking a stampede among the spectators for an early copy of the newspaper.

Engine #573 was cut out and a depot engine drew the train across the bridge to the Alleghany River station, where the train stopped for seven minutes while the air brakes were adjusted. The car inspectors examined the wheels and failed to find a single overheated journal or pin.

Locomotive Engine #26 (G. Tabor, engineer), took over in Pittsburgh. The engine was handsomely festooned with deer antlers and flags. An additional supply of ice was taken aboard to refrigerate the fresh produce and fruits. A curious crowd watched the steward open the trap door beneath the hotel car to load the ice. Thereafter, the locomotive whistle sounded, and the passengers scrambled on board — **2,865 miles to San Francisco.**

The train was now switched onto the tracks of the Pittsburgh, Fort Wayne and Chicago Railroad, irreverently known as the "Pig's feet, Whiskey and Cigar Line," soon to be a lessee of the Pennsylvania Railroad. The company was founded in 1859 by the amalgamation of railroad lines extending westward from Fort Wayne to Chicago and eastward from Fort Wayne to Pittsburgh. The company operated a single track, an arrangement which would be retained for another twelve years. This single track made it imperative that station and trackmen maintain absolute vigilance to ensure that the track would be cleared of on-coming traffic. The Jarrett-Palmer Express was now a designated "hot shot" train, with a "high ball" signal (absolute priority).

A gravel and cinder road now replaced the macadam bed of the Pennsylvania. Except for straight stretches, the ride was not as smooth as the Pennsylvania. Excitement began to take its toll on the passengers. Few bothered to look out of the window when the engineer sounded the whistle to indicate that they had left Pennsylvania and were crossing into Ohio. The train passed the border at East Palestine, Ohio, at 12:12 P.M., one minute behind schedule.

Along the way, crowds of people lined the road, or stood on house tops and fences to watch the train pass. At 12:38 P.M., the passengers saw other trains dutifully switched onto the sidings.

Instructions had been issued to ensure that all traffic yielded twenty minutes to the Jarrett and Palmer Transcontinental Express. Speed increased as they made the straight run past Woodland, Damascus, and Heloit, Ohio.

Alliance, Ohio, was reached three minutes ahead of schedule. Here another locomotive stood by with engineer John Vanwormers at the throttle. This would be the first of four engine stops on the Chicago run, in addition to the several operating stops to take on coal and water. It took less than thirty seconds to replace the engine, and they were again underway. At first, the travelers were puzzled at the sight of empty factories and deserted schoolhouses, until they realized that the occupants were all outdoors lining the tracks! Crestline, Ohio, was reached at 3:50 P.M., five minutes ahead of schedule. Locomotives were again changed and *Engine #199* (A. Kelker, engineer), substituted.

From Crestline, the road ran "straight as a beeline," and the speed of the rocking train reached fifty miles per hour. Trees danced in the distance and the luxuriant countryside delighted the eye. A refreshing breeze relieved the oppressive heat, but off in the distance the passengers saw an ominous gathering of dark clouds. Mr. Williams, the *Herald* correspondent, showed them the dire storm predictions which had appeared in the morning edition of his newspaper. Weather changes were matters of grave concern to the trainmen, but they kept their worries to themselves. From Crestline to Fort Wayne, the 131 miles was traversed in two hours and fifty-five minutes. Off to a siding, they saw the passengers of the Chicago Express glumly watching as the Jarrett-Palmer Express raced by.

Fort Wayne, Indiana, was reached at 6:55 P.M. Large throngs crowded the station. Railroad men called the city "the Altoona of

Thursday, June 1   33

the West," referring to its large repair and construction shop. Fortunately, repairs on the Jarrett-Palmer Express were not then required. The train remained ten minutes in Fort Wayne, sufficient time to offload the *Herald.* At 7:05 P.M. they started out with *Engine #221,* (A. H. Polliemus, engineer) on a clear track to Chicago. The conductor announced that they would try to reach the city by 10:00 P.M. After leaving Fort Wayne, the train had regained lost time by irregularly achieving speeds of over a mile a minute. The situation changed suddenly when a blinding rainstorm struck, accompanied by bursts of lightning and thunder, which slowed travel to an agonizing crawl for the next thirty miles. Happily, the storm was less severe then had been feared. The average speed from Pittsburgh had been 42.1 miles per hour.

Chicago, the second authorized stop, was reached at 10:00 P.M., **twenty-one hours and thirty-six minutes from New York** and twenty-five minutes ahead of schedule. (In 2006, the similar Amtrak run takes twenty-two hours, forty-five minutes). A station change was not required. During his transcontinental trip in 1879, Robert Louis Stevenson complained that he was sorely inconvenienced in Chicago by having to take an omnibus to another station. Fortunately, the passengers of the Jarrett-Palmer Express were spared this nuisance. Chicago had been severely burned in the Great Fire of 1871, with a third of its 118,000 residents left homeless; but the city had since been rebuilt. So much so, that Stevenson, who had contributed sixpence towards the reconstruction of Chicago after the great fire, felt that his donation should have been refunded.

An immense crowd stood in the heavy rain on the Madison Street depot, with thirty policemen on hand to maintain order. People had learned of the express train by word of mouth and had come to see it, some from as far as twenty miles, although no special effort had been made to recruit spectators. For them, the Jarrett-Palmer Express was not merely a record-breaking transcontinental train journey, but a patriotic expression of the national celebration. Wrote the *Herald* correspondent:

> If Mr. Jarrett succeeds in reaching San Francisco according to the scheduled time, the fact will revolutionize our present system of railway travel and make rapid passenger trains necessary.

At Chicago, General Porter left the train, along with some other passengers. To the reporters, Porter issued the pronouncement that he was "well satisfied" with the trip. The *Herald* bundles were quickly offloaded and, once again, caused a sensation. For the first time the citizens of Chicago could read the *New York Herald* on the evening of its day of publication.

Departure was delayed for ten minutes while the train took on ice. The passengers were permitted to detrain for a few minutes to stretch their legs, but had to rush back when the steam whistle sounded. The train was switched to the Chicago and North Western Railroad system, and Augustus H. Preston next took the throttle.

Three rail systems ran from Chicago to Council Bluffs, Iowa, the shortest route operated by the Chicago and North Western Railroad. The company was chartered in 1859 and had an extensive Midwestern network. Built with considerable English capital, the company was said to have an English outlook in its operation, by which was meant that it made no improvements until it had the cash in hand.

Promptly at 10:45 P.M., the train left the Chicago station. **2,396 miles to San Francisco.** The passengers would once again be traveling on an active one-track system. A total of thirty-seven trains would have to be sidetracked or diverted throughout the trip. The engineer was instructed to reach the Mississippi River by 1:00 A.M.

FRIDAY, JUNE 2

AFTER A STRAIGHT and uneventful run of 138 miles, they approached Fulton, Illinois, on the Mississippi River, at 12:58 A.M. Across the river was Clinton, Iowa. Thus far they had been traveling **twenty-three hours and sixty-six minutes** from Jersey City. The passengers were exhausted and had long since taken to their berths, which had been hurriedly prepared, as best as could be done at breakneck speed. No one was awake when the train slowed to six miles per hour and began creeping across the mile-long Chicago and North Western Bridge spanning the Mississippi River.

Later, the conductor informed the travelers that a large crowd had been on hand to loudly cheer them on.

They now entered the Iowa division of the road, and the *Hookset* (Thomas Keefe, engineer) replaced the present engine. This was to be the first of four engine changes on the Chicago and North Western Railroad in addition to five operating stops. The train gained a few minutes on the 116-mile run to Belle Plaine, Iowa, but lost twenty minutes when a branch pump on the engine ruptured. The *W. A. Booth* (John Jackson, engineer) replaced the damaged engine and off they sped. Boone Station, Iowa, was reached at 6:31 A.M., where *L. Holbrook* (Philip Pickering, engineer) was hooked on. They arrived at Dunlap, Iowa, a distance of 102 miles, in two hours and nineteen minutes.

Here another engine, the *Charles Dow* (John Boynsenn, engineer) was substituted. Some of the four locomotive changes were made to forestall an engine breakdown; others, for the convenience of the crew, so as not to bring them too far afield from their home base.

Mile after mile of tall prairie grass sped by until at last, forty minutes ahead of schedule, the passengers caught their first glimpse of low cliffs, as Council Bluffs on the Missouri River came into view. Thus far, the average speed from New York had been forty-two miles per hour, and the fastest time on the Chicago and North Western Railroad was sixty-two miles per hour! At 10:00 A.M., the train pulled into the transfer station at Council Bluffs. The city derived its name from the pow-wow held by Lewis and Clark with the Mahas Indians on the high ground overlooking the native village. Overland travelers knew the place as Kanesville. The train halted at the Missouri River and the trainmen filled the tanks of the Pullman car with the muddy Missouri water. A few mischievous passengers tried to convince the British that they were taking on beer.

The train crawled at six miles per hour along the three miles of flood plain approaches and across the bridge. Built in 1872, the Union Pacific railroad bridge was nearly 2,750 feet long, with a clearance of sixty feet above medium low water of the Missouri River, to allow boats to safely pass below. Since the bridge had no floor planking, wagons could not pass over it. Before the bridge was built, a ferry carried the train across the river and in winter, trains crossed on an ice bridge.

Omaha (elevation 966 feet), on the west bank, was an important scheduled stop. With a population of 20,000, Omaha could claim the largest smelting plant in the United States, as well as seven breweries, a car works, foundries and three well-established newspapers. No less than 10,000 freight cars passed through the city in 1875. The travel books pronounced it "the grand gateway through which the eastern tide of travel and immigration is passing." The Crash of 1857 had brought hard times to the city, but its economy revived two years later with the discovery of gold in Colorado.

Overflow crowds jammed the station. The mayor was on hand and was formally presented with copy of the *Herald*. Local pressmen scurried aboard the train to interview Mr. Williams, the *Herald* reporter. Throngs of poorly and curiously clothed immigrants lounged around the train station. Three rail systems brought these people to Omaha from all parts of the East, where they collected, while awaiting transportation westward on special emigrant trains.

At Omaha, the Union Pacific took over. The company had been chartered by the federal government in 1863 to build 1,000 miles of track from Omaha through largely unsettled land. Initially, they were hampered by a stretched supply line and hostile warriors, then, by the challenge of the mountains.

For the rest of the trip, the train again would be riding on a one-track bed. **Omaha to San Francisco, 1,882 miles!** Passengers were instructed by the guide books to prepare themselves for five hundred miles of plains to Cheyenne, Wyoming; five hundred miles of Rockies to Ogden, Utah; five hundred miles of American desert to Reno, Nevada, and lastly two hundred miles over the Sierra Nevada to San Francisco. The train people had their own awesome perspective: a five-thousand-foot climb over the Rockies in the next five hundred miles; later, a two-thousand-foot climb to the summit of the Sierra Nevada in fifty miles.

They left Omaha at 10:10 A.M. on *Locomotive #146* (E. B. Wood, engineer). It, too, was a 4-4-0, and, like the succeeding engines that would take them to Cheyenne, it had sixteen-inch by twenty-

Across the Plains. [Central Pacific R. R. Photographic History Museum, Sacramento, CA.]

four-inch cylinders, five-foot eight-inch drivers and weighed thirty-three tons. A member of the local press accompanied the train for a few miles while he concluded his interviews. The journey which began at the Nebraska bottomlands continued along the rolling prairies of the Platte Valley, with tall, six-foot grass waving in the wind. The Elkhorn River was crossed at 10:46 A.M. Travel guides reported that the river was bountifully stocked with pike, pickerel, bass, perch, and sunfish, thanks to a sudden freshet which had earlier hurled from a bridge a railroad car carrying a load of fish eggs. Passing through a deep cut, they met up with the Platte River and began to follow its northern bank. The grade had been slowly rising ten feet to the mile, but the passengers took no note of it.

Along the way, the Union Pacific had rights to two hundred feet of land on each side of the track. Moreover, it had been given alternate sections of vacant land, ten sections to the mile, for ten miles on each side (mineral rights excepted). Some of the land had been developed; some had passed into the hands of speculators and most awaited the arrival of new waves of wide-eyed emigrants. In years gone by, this area had been regarded as part of the "Great American Desert," but as agriculture took hold in this rich alluvial basin, the appellation had been revised.

Even during the daylight hours, the party was exhausted. At every town, cries of "God speed" were heard. The Union Pacific maintained fifty-one stations, separated by an average of fourteen miles, and it seemed that at every station people had turned out to greet them. The ride was smooth along the Platte Valley, despite their breakneck speed of fifty miles per hour. Everywhere, flowers were in full bloom. An unending row of telegraph poles lined the track, attracting hoards of woodpeckers. Until a few years ago, buffalo had used the poles as scratching posts to help them shed their hump manes at the approach of summer; but with the pending extermination of that animal, there were fewer calls to replace uprooted poles. Cottonwood trees grew along the river, but away from the banks, there was little forestation. Most of the original timber had been cut to provide ties for railroad construction, and what few trees were visible, had been recently planted as windbreaks for the farms. The newly arrived farmer first broke sod for a corn field, then planted trees for a timber shelter. According to the travel books, the shallow Platte River ("a mile wide, an inch deep") under-drained the valley, permitting sufficient water to be retained, even during the dry season, thus insuring a good crop.

    The train rushed along the Platte River, making the most of the flat grade. Every object on the train rattled. Shaving with a straight "cut-throat" razor was hazardous, and passengers had long since resigned themselves to whisker stubble.

    At Columbus, Nebraska (elevation 1,432 feet), they saw the eastbound Pacific Express off on a siding. Columbus had become an important agricultural seat. Thanks to the railroad, grain was no longer being used just for cattle feed but was now a cash crop. Further on, antelope scurried across the plains, but however hard the passengers strained their eyes, they could see nothing of the vaunted buffalo. Gone were the days when travelers were encouraged to fire their revolvers through an open window at the shaggy creatures.

    They arrived at Grand Island, Nebraska (elevation 1,850 feet), at 11:48 A.M., where they spent eighteen minutes changing engines and taking on fresh water for the kitchen. Apparently the toilets had a separate tank, for when the passengers went to wash their hands, yellow water gushed from the tap. This was the

Friday, June 2 43

"beer" that had been taken aboard at the Missouri River. Grand Island had a population of 1,500, mostly thrifty German farmers who were prospering handsomely on the rich alluvial soil of the Platte. They were said to be already producing twenty-five to thirty bushels of grain to the acre.

Engine #156 (W. Lloyd, engineer) had been built in 1869 by Hinkley and Williams and had the same configuration and driver diameter as the preceding. The train pulled out at 2:03 P.M. With Grand Island behind them, an unbounded vista of untilled prairie spread out to the horizon. Wild sunflowers grew around the depots to a height of nine feet, but diminished in size as the train moved westward. Along the tracks were ruts made in bygone years by the endless line of emigrant wagons but now overgrown and fallen into disuse. Kearney, Nebraska, was swiftly passed. It was here that Passpartout, Mr. Phineas Fogg's valet, was kidnapped by the Sioux in Jules Verne's *Around the World in Ninety Days*. A few stations west of Kearney was Plum Creek, where nine years before, a party of Cheyenne derailed a train and killed eleven trainmen. Several crumbling, long-abandoned forts were a reminder of the overland years. From this point westward, in the old days, the Sioux and Northern Cheyenne had given the railroad unremitting trouble.

Willow Island, Nebraska (elevation 2,511 feet), 250 miles from Omaha, was reached at 4:15 P.M. They were now on the one-hundredth meridian, halfway across the continent, having traveled 1,645 miles in **thirty-nine hours and twelve minutes,** at an average speed of forty-two miles per hour. As they sped along the plains, the passengers had difficulty estimating their speed, since there were few trees to furnish a point of reference. Desolate sod houses and white sun-bleached barns were the sole evidence of settlement; yet crowds appeared at all the stations, drawn from far and wide. Bonfires were lit at every road crossing. So monotonous had the crowds become that the passengers no longer put aside their books or papers to wave to them.

Along the Platte, the train made one run of seventy-nine miles in seventy-five minutes and another run of forty-five miles in forty-four minutes! Such speeds were hitherto unimaginable, since speed limits previously had been vigorously enforced. Eleven sidetracked trains were passed. Thus far, the passengers thankfully had been spared the hazards of prairie fires and of grasshopper invasions, which might have caused hours of delay—or worse. They passed Chimney Rock, a three-hundred-foot natural column, and a landmark for the Oregon travelers. North Platte, Nebraska (elevation 2,789 feet), was reached at 5:15 P.M., two hours, twenty-seven minutes ahead of schedule. Here, *Locomotive #77* (Carl Pierce, engineer), awaited them. It had been built by Rogers in 1868 with similar configuration and dimensions as the Omaha engine. The station was an important railroad center, with complete railroad facilities and stalls for twenty cars. Fortunately, repairs were not then required.

After leaving the town of North Platte, they followed the swift and muddy South Platte River. Toward dusk, the passengers filed into the dining section for their evening meal, but at speeds of fifty miles per hour, the service was less than exemplary.

As the soil became parched and heavily impregnated with alkali, stock raising began to supplant agriculture, and buffalo grass replaced tall grass. Stockmen had found that short buffalo grass was as nutritious for their cattle as it had been for buffalo. Hay was not required in winter, since according to the guide books, the cattle could well live off the rich buffalo grass.

Friday, June 2

Soon they left Nebraska and dipped briefly into Colorado at Julesburg (elevation 3,500 feet), once called "the wickedest city in America." Julesburg had been an important stop for the Pony Express and was now a way station for the shipment of cattle, as well as a point of departure for the Black Hill mines of Montana. The train quickly reentered Nebraska, following another branch of the South Platte River to Sidney, Nebraska (elevation 4,073 feet), a town of a few hundred people. At Sidney, the train slowed, since they were by now three hours and fifty-two minutes ahead of schedule. Cowboys galloped alongside the cars and fired their revolvers in a merry salute (*feu de joie*).

Here in Sidney, the passengers caught their first glimpse of Indians at the train stations, which henceforth would be a frequent sight. The Indian women offered for sale blankets, pottery and trinkets, while the warriors, according to the guidebooks, lounged around the stations "with scalps dangling from their waists." One of the trainmen might have pointed the spot where six years previously, a train had been attacked by warriors, but had made good its escape.

The Union Pacific had fought the Sioux warriors for every mile of road construction. The Central Pacific, on the other hand, avoided attacks by giving lifetime passes to the Shoshone and Cheyenne chiefs, and by allowing warriors to ride free of charge in the baggage cars. With the Apaches and Paiutes, the company won them over with gifts of money.

After Sidney, buffalo grass dominated the landscape. Mile after mile of prairie dog villages extended up to the very road bed. The little creatures stood fearlessly on their hind feet and watched the approach of the train, before darting into their bolt holes. Toward dusk, the train climbed to 6,000 feet, as it passed into Wyoming. For the first time, passengers glimpsed the Rocky

Mountains in the distance and began to notice the rarified air. So fast was the train moving along the "bewildering curves" and "sudden grades," that the *Herald* correspondent had difficulty composing his dispatches.

They arrived at 10:40 P.M. in Cheyenne, Wyoming, "The Magic City of the Plains" (elevation 6,044 feet), heralded by an brilliant barrage from rockets and Roman candles which Mr. Jarrett had distributed to the passengers. The spectators cheered so loudly that the band could scarcely be heard.

Cheyenne had begun as a railroad "hell on wheels" town, but had since sufficiently matured so that it could now boast of five churches and twenty gambling saloons. Situated on the most easterly spur of the Rocky Mountains, Cheyenne was the largest town between Omaha and Salt Lake City, having a population of 1,500.

The train halted for a few minutes while a new locomotive, *#168* (Nicholas Weeks, engineer), was coupled on. The engine, built by Taunton in 1875, was a 4-4-0 with eighteen-inch by twenty-four-inch cylinders, had five-foot eight-inch drivers, and, like all the subsequent engines which would take them to Ogden, weighed thirty-three tons.

The crowd called on Jarrett and Barrett to make a speech, but their declamations were cut short by the train whistle. William Allen now took the throttle. A nineteen-year-old tramp is said to have boarded the train in Cheyenne and climbed onto the roof of one of the cars. As the train increased its speed, the man held on to the stove pipe for dear life. The cinders from the engine chimney burned his clothing and tore at his body and face.

The lore of the railroad tramp was still in its infancy. A knowledgeable tramp usually climbed *under* the car and coiled up along the ironwork between the wheels, half-lying and

Friday, June 2

half-hanging as he was carried along, six inches above the tracks. Railroads had been having increasing difficulties with these people. Trainmen insisted on calling them "tramps" (or worse), reserving the word "hobo" for itinerant train workers. The term "hobo" was derived from the itinerant hoe boy, who rented out his services at harvest time.

The route before them had been surveyed in 1865 by General Grenville Dodge while he was still in the army fighting the Crow Nation. It was Dodge who chose the Mormon route, rather than the Oregon Trail or the route of the Forty-Niners. He rejected South Pass (Oregon Trail), as undependable in winter, choosing instead a long ridge ("Lone Tree Pass") through the Black Hills (of Wyoming) that led up to Sherman Summit.

The train began to climb the Laramie Mountains, which had a grade of ninety feet to the mile. The services of a helper engine were scornfully refused. It slowly passed a stretch of granite boulders, spotted with yellow moss, and ascended to Sherman Summit (elevation 8,400 feet) on the world's highest railroad track. Most of the passengers were fast asleep and missed this memorable experience. Those who remained awake had the feeling that they were riding on a high plateau, rather than over lofty mountains. Sherman Summit was the highest point in the Black Hills, an outlying eastern range of the Rockies. The Continental Divide lay two hundred miles to the west and was one thousand feet lower.

In a blink of an eye they crossed the 650-foot Dale River Bridge, "one of the wonders of the transcontinental route," according to the guide books.

SATURDAY, JUNE 3

L ARAMIE CITY WAS REACHED at 12:03 A.M., where the hobo was summarily removed from his perch. In six minutes, *Engine #167* (William Allen, engineer), built by Taunton in 1875, was coupled to the train and off they sped. A total of eight locomotives would be used by the Union Pacific in the run from Omaha to Ogden. The train would maintain an average speed of forty-one miles per hour and reach a maximum speed of seventy-two miles per hour!

They left Laramie over a wooden truss bridge. The appearance of sagebrush and rolling prairie gave indication that they were approaching the Laramie Plains, which ran west for one hundred miles.

Cooper Lake, Wyoming (elevation 7,044 feet), was reached in eleven minutes, and Rock Creek, fifty-one miles from Laramie, in exactly one hour. Large windmills were seen in Laramie and in many other stations, some as high as seventy-five feet, which were used to pump water into the thirty-foot water tanks. Snow sheds began to appear. These, together with snow fences and raised track, protected the track from snowdrifts.

The train climbed the heavily wooded slopes, uneventfully crossing the Continental Divide. Hardly anyone was awake to take notice. At Medicine Bow, Wyoming, they made an operating stop. Since the water here was strongly alkaline, the firemen had to be especially vigilant, lest corrosion form inside the boiler, pipes or water pumps. In a station where the water was unusable, the station water tank would have to have been previously filled from a water train.

During these operating stops, the brakeman carefully inspected the car wheels to ensure that the journal boxes were free of smoke or flame. The journal box was a metal box placed around the axle bearing, which contained a pad saturated with a lubricant. If, during his rounds, the brakeman detected nothing amiss, he called *"All black!"* If he observed smoke or flames, then the "hot box" would have to be replaced, or additional oil packing or "dope" inserted into it. Otherwise, the heat generated by the friction might melt the bearings or cause the axle to fracture. These events could cause a fire (the cars were made of wood) or a major derailment. The Union Pacific encountered six such hot boxes during its run, which fortunately could be corrected at the operating stops.

After a quick watering, the train was again on its way. Sagebrush now dominated the landscape as far as the eye could see. The guide books informed the reader that sagebrush was an excellent source of nourishment for antelope and sheep. Three hours out from Laramie, they arrived in Rawlins, Wyoming (elevation 6,732 feet), at 3:09 A.M. Here in 1867, General John Rawlins, the former chief of staff to General Grant, was attacked by a party of Cheyenne while out for an early ride and narrowly escaped with his scalp. Nearby were several coal mines. Unfortunately, their coal was lignite, which, unlike bituminous, did not "coke" and was therefore unsuited for the engine firebox.

At Rawlins, they took on *Engine #151* (Robert Miller, engineer), built by Taunton in 1875, which would carry them on their ascent. So skillfully was the roadbed laid out that the train seemed to climb effortlessly; but, in fact, the engines were working hard.

An anxious lookout was kept for weather changes, since sudden rain could swiftly imperil the road bed. After completing a run of seventy-five miles in 120 minutes, they arrived at Bitter Creek, Wyoming.

Wyoming was long regarded a part of the mysterious "Great American Desert," as was any region devoid of trees. In Nebraska, settlement and irrigation had impressively shrunk the pale of desolation, but in Wyoming the "desert" appeared unyielding. Only jackrabbits and lizards seemed to thrive. Wrote one traveler in 1869: "A vast barren basin utterly destitute of life, devoid of living streams, truly the Valley of the Shadow of Death."

Rock Springs was passed, an unattractive town of dugouts and shanties. Six trains had to be diverted during the run. As the sun came up, they entered a canyon and approached Green River Station, Wyoming (elevation 6,140 feet), at 6:20 A.M., where in three minutes Taunton *Engine #169* was substituted, and Frank Hutchins took the throttle. Green River, Wyoming, was an adobe town, which derived its name from the color imparted to the river by the shale. The Green River joins the Colorado for a wild passage down the Grand Canyon, recently described by Major John Wesley Powell.

The train left Green River, Wyoming, at 6:27 A.M., six hours and fifty minutes ahead of schedule. It passed through several deep cuts where numerous fossils were embedded in the walls. The train stopped at Bridger, Wyoming (elevation 6,780 feet), for water. Here, a well-wisher presented Jarrett with a string of mountain trout. From the windows on the left side of the train, the passengers could glimpse the spectacular Uintah Mountains in the distance. They climbed from 6,140 feet up to 7,835 feet and down to 6,820 feet, maintaining an average speed of 40.8 miles per hour.

On through the Bad Lands they sped, marveling at the innumerable fossils embedded in the horizontal strata of sandstone. Fossils were enjoying great attention in the two decades following the publication of Darwin's *Origin of the Species*. Independence Rock was passed, a landmark venerated by the overland travelers. Eleven snow sheds were counted along the way.

Evanston, Wyoming (elevation 6,835 feet), was reached at 9:05 A.M. and *Locomotive #153*, also of Taunton manufacture, was substituted. Doc Reynolds took the throttle. Thus far, they had traveled 2,357 miles from New York in **fifty-six hours and two minutes**.

Evanston had a picturesque setting, with the Bear River on one side and the large divide on the other. The passengers saw the shacks and houses of the Chinese laborers who initially had worked for the Central Pacific and were now employed by the Union Pacific to maintain the roadbed. Coal mined in the region yielded fifty percent coke, which was welcomed by the railroad, but, unfortunately, the mines had caught fire. The editors of the *Evanston Age* came aboard the train and were each presented with a copy of the *Herald*.

The passengers used the operating stop to sit down to their morning breakfast. To their delight, they were served a special cuisine of mountain trout and antelope steaks, in addition to their usual fare.

Suddenly, the Evanston telegrapher rushed in with word of a wash-out forty miles ahead in Weber Canyon! A deep gloom settled over the party. The news devastated Jarrett. This one mishap could irrevocably frustrate all his hopes and carefully formulated plans. Ogden, Utah, notified Jarrett that it was prepared to dis-

Saturday, June 3

patch a train, if necessary, to collect the passengers from the other side of the wash-out. After the engine change had been completed, they left Evanston and entered Utah, to begin the challenging ascent up the Wasatch Mountains.

The tracks ran around abrupt curves, past gullies and curious rock formations. The passengers stared with deep foreboding at the patches of snow and huge boulders. They continued on through a 770-foot blue sandstone tunnel and entered spectacular Echo Canyon, seven miles long and three-quarters mile wide. As they passed downgrade to the foot of the rugged canyon, they marveled at the red stone cliffs, broken into weird shaft-like pinnacles, spires and towers, many of which had been given names, which by now were quite familiar to tourists. Echo River was crossed and re-crossed thirty times. Eight miles down track they entered Weber Canyon, of comparable beauty, which narrows at the site of the venerable "Thousand Mile Tree." The tree marks the halfway point between Omaha and Sacramento. Nearby is Devil's Slide, a narrow tract of two parallel granite outcroppings, attached to the side of the mountain.

Abruptly, a track man appeared up ahead, holding a red flag. The train slowed as it approached the site of the recent washout. Wading up to their waists in the roiling flood was a gang of Chinese laborers, who were strenuously engaged in pulling up brush and earth, and using the material to shore up a temporary track, called a "shoo fly," which, with extraordinary perseverance, they had managed to construct. A voyager describes these faithful workers as "bare-legged, ragged, and dressed in a sort of hybrid mixture of Chinese and Caucasian styles, with their pig tails twisted up out of the way and their great straw hats tied under their chins." Thanks to their exertions, the train could by-pass the washout.

Thousand Mile Tree, Weber Valley.
[Central Pacific R. R. Photographic History Museum, Sacramento, CA.]

Although Chinese laborers now maintained the Union Pacific roadbed, early construction from Echo Valley to Promontory Point had been performed by a work force of 4,000 Mormons, who had been left idle by a grasshopper plague. Brigham Young put them to work for the Union Pacific in return for the payment of two million dollars to the Church and an agreement to transport Mormon immigrants at reduced rates.

Once past the "shoo fly," the train was given the "high ball" signal to resume speed. It crossed the Weber River on the famous trestle bridge, which had been constructed in one week with 180,000 feet of timber. In this very region in 1869, a similar washout had delayed for two days the arrival of the Union Pacific train at the Promontory Point ceremonies, but fortunately, a repair was made and the ceremonies could proceed.

They emerged from Devil's Gap in the mountains and came onto the Great Salt Lake Valley, with Ogden (elevation 4,301 feet) appearing in the distance like an oasis in the desert. Despite the washout, they had made the run in eighty minutes, and arrived in Ogden at 10:30 A.M., **fifty-seven hours fifty-six minutes from New York.**

Ogden was an important station for the Union Pacific and the Central Pacific railroads, both of which shared the advantages of a prosperous city. Ogden had machine and repair shops and numerous foundries, which made use of the iron ore mined in the region.

The land had been under Mexican sovereignty in 1841, when the Mormons first trekked from Nauvoo, Illinois, to the Utah Territory; but by 1848 it had been acquired by the United States under the terms of the Treaty of Guadeloupe Hidalgo at the close of the Mexican War. Meanwhile, the Mormons had set up the State of Deseret, which the government of the United States disavowed and instead organized the Utah Territory, with Brigham Young, as territorial governor. The region prospered beyond the founders' fondest hopes. Thanks to a fine system of irrigation and a benevolent climate, annual yields of sixty (!) bushels of wheat were not uncommon, absent locusts and drought.

The official junction of the Union Pacific and Central Pacific lines was initially at Promontory Point, fifty miles west of Ogden. Later, desperate to reach the prosperous city, the Central Pacific bought the intervening track from Union Pacific and moved the operating demarcation to Ogden.

The Central Pacific Railroad had been incorporated in 1861 to construct a rail line over the Sierra Nevada Mountains in California and thence to meet up with the Union Pacific. The gigantic project was drawn up and kept alive by four venturesome business men: Leland Stanford, Collis P. Huntington, Mark Hopkins and Charles Crocker; and a remarkable engineer, Theodore D. Judah, all of whom, regardless of their faults, have earned a respected place in the railroad Pantheon.

At Ogden, the train was switched to the Utah central branch of the Central Pacific. Eighty bundles of the *Herald* were thrown onto the platform, creating a grand scramble. Sacks of mail for Ogden were offloaded and letters for San Francisco taken on board. It was in Ogden that passengers, given sufficient time, would buy gold, since greenbacks were not welcome in California. Also, here the Central Pacific would usually cut out the Pullman cars and substitute their own rolling stock, but by prior arrangements, the Pullman Palace Hotel was allowed to continue.

Locomotive #149 now took over and would continue all the way to Oakland, California. Unlike the Pennsylvania *#573* engine, Central Pacific's *#149* would later require the aid of helper engines. The passengers, who had seen the necessity of frequent engine changes on the Chicago and North Western and the Union Pacific runs, knew nothing of Central Pacific's insistence on a single engine. Later, the *Herald* correspondent wrote about the decision: "It was a risk experiment, and none of the party could care to assist in another such demonstration of mechanical power.... None of the party knew...that the experiment was a dangerous one." This decision to rely on one engine would later cost the Central Pacific delays; but the consequences might have been worse. In the cab of *#149* were engineers Henry Small and

James Wright and Chief Engineer Benjamin Smith, in addition to three firemen. All six remained with the train and took turns at the throttle or firebox. They spent their free time in the commissary car.

Locomotive #149, Black Fox (H. Small, engineer), was a McQueen thirty-three-ton, eight-wheeler with five-foot drivers and sixteen-inch by twenty-four-inch cylinders, capable of generating 145 pounds of steam pressure. It was built in 1868 by Schenectady Locomotive. While in Ogden, the trainmen inspected the brake shoes of the Pullman car and found that some were worn and sticky. Since the Central Pacific lacked compatible replacements, the management would meet the problem by later adding three air brake coaches, so that the train could be slowed.

The train left Ogden at 10:44 A.M. **Ogden to San Francisco 883 miles!** The roadbed lay north of the Great Salt Lake bypassing Salt Lake City, to Brigham Young's eternal regret. After crossing the Ogden River on a pile bridge, the engineer received a report that a hot box had developed on the wheels of the baggage car. He reduced speed but did not stop the train. The trainman knelt on a step of the baggage car and, hanging onto the guard rail with one hand, he removed the cover of the journal box and inserted hot dope, oil and wipes. Speed could then be resumed.

They followed the flat shoreline of Great Salt Lake for forty miles, before beginning their climb up the Promontory Range. On they sped over heavy grades, around short curves and through deep rocky cuts, crossing a 550-foot wooden trestle bridge over Blue Creek. To the left of the track, they saw verdant farms, watered by ingenious irrigation systems. For a short distance, the grade was 110 feet to the mile. Despite the hot box interlude, the fifty-four miles from Ogden to Promontory (elevation 4,905 feet) was completed in sixty-nine minutes.

The town of Promontory, now of only historical importance, was situated between two ridges of the Promontory Range. At one time, the town held the record of twenty-eight violent deaths in a single month. Here in 1869, the Union Pacific was linked to the Central Pacific in a colorful ceremony. Before then, the Central Pacific had been racing eastward toward profitable Ogden and the Union Pacific had been laying handsomely subsidized track westward, so that for some distance (250 miles?) the tracks ran parallel to each other and sometimes within hailing distance! Congress put a stop to this wasteful nonsense by demanding a junction, whereupon both companies hastily complied.

The prostitutes and gamblers, who constituted the majority of those that clung to the declining fortunes of Promontory, showed up at high noon to cheer the Jarrett-Palmer Express as it whizzed by. Three miles from Promontory, they passed a sign proclaiming "Ten Mile Track." Here on April 29, 1869, an unbelievable ten miles of track had been laid in one day by the Central Pacific's Chinese and Irish laborers.

A desolate country lay ahead, stretching interminably through Utah and Nevada. To the left they saw waves of Great Salt Lake dashing onto the rocks along the shore. Kelton, Utah (elevation 4,222 feet), on the northwest corner of the Great Salt Lake, was reached at 11:42 A.M. As they came to a stop, the brake pipe broke on the Pullman car. This was a perilous situation, since ahead lay the most challenging part of the journey. Handbrakes on the Pullman would henceforth have to be used to arrest the speed of that car.

No sooner were they underway, when another hot box developed. Fortunately, Benjamin Smith, the chief engineer, could correct it without the duty engineer having to stop the train. As they wound around the side of the mountain, the Great Salt Lake disappeared, and in its place, the alkali plain of the Great American Desert hove into view. Few of the travelers could fully appreciate the suffering of the overland travelers who made the perilous journey.

They crossed into Nevada and saw a land even more barren than the one they had left. "Of all the desolate land we have traveled, Nevada may be the worst yet. I cannot imagine that a drop of dew has ever lain on this God-forsaken land," wrote one traveler. At Toano, Nevada (elevation 5,973 feet), they stopped to take on coal. Workmen ran up the newly-constructed ramp with bushels of coal and dumped them in the tender. On the other side of the ramp, men carried buckets of water and emptied them in the water tank. Barrows of coal were brought to the baggage car and loaded from underneath. The operating stop took but four minutes! At Wells, Nevada, the Salt Lake trainmen left and the Humboldt men came on. They, in turn, would leave later at Truckee, California, to be replaced by the Sacramento & Western team. Although lately forgotten, Wells has an important spring nearby that refreshed the desperate overlanders. Twenty-two miles later, the train crossed the summit of the Humboldt Range at 6,548 feet and entered the long valley of the Humboldt River.

Guidebooks kept the readers informed about the stations and natural features that they were approaching. Interesting stories were related about the most seemingly lackluster surroundings.

Elko, Nevada (elevation 5,096 feet), was reached at 4:30 P.M. At the time, it was the most important town in Nevada and the most prominent station of the Central Pacific, east of Sacramento. Elko had gained renown for the medicinal properties of its six mineral springs, which were also used to hatch chicken eggs. Around the station, the traveler could see Indian women with their crimson faces striped with yellow paint.

They left Elko to begin a three-hundred-mile run along the Humboldt River. Once again, only the monotonous sagebrush seemed to thrive. The train reached a breathtaking speed of fifty-five miles per hour. At Carlin, Nevada (elevation 4,903 feet), another railroad town, they paused to greet a sidetracked eastbound train. Several of the eastbound passengers pleaded for a copy of the *Herald*, which Mr. Williams was pleased to supply. The condition of *Engine #149* was beginning to cause concern. Ahead lay the most dangerous part of the journey, but whatever the obstacles, the Central Pacific was determined to run the *#149* all the way to the end. The passengers could not then appreciate the danger. Because of the faulty brake shoes on the Pullman, speed had to be slowed on heavily descending grades, to keep the engineer from losing control.

The train followed the Humboldt River around sharp curves and heavy grades, winding around the base of the bluffs with the river flowing below them. Innumerable snow sheds were passed. Fifty miles past Humboldt Wells, the snow-peaked tops of the Ruby Range came into view. At an insignificant station called Beowawe, they caught a fleeting glimpse of the grave of an early overland woman. Out of respect for her hardships, the station men had adopted the grave, fenced it off and reverently attended to the grave marker. On they sped along a crooked roadbed, through cuts and gorges with perpendicular walls. Occasionally, a squalid Shoshone village could be seen.

They came to Battle Mountain, Nevada (elevation 4,517 feet), a one-street town, where they stopped for eighteen minutes

Saturday, June 3

to take on coal and water. A defective journal box was cooled and a replacement installed. Thereafter, they had a straight run for twenty miles across the plain. Small villages of Paiute Indians could be seen. The Paiutes were widely renowned as fishermen and hunters. According to the guidebooks, their women could faultlessly stitch handsome rabbit coats. They followed the Humboldt River in a slowly descending grade along several valleys, nestled between the mountain ranges. Low alkali flats, whitened with salt, extended for miles in all directions.

Winnemucca, Nevada, was reached at 8:20 P.M., **474 miles from San Francisco!** A large crowd of Paiute Indians was camped near the train station. The train by now was estimated to be nine hours and twenty minutes ahead of schedule. Engineer Rice next took over the *#149* for a 136-mile run.

The desert hamlet of Humboldt (elevation 4,236 feet) was swiftly passed. They continued the descent to Mirage, so named for the reflection of the sun on the gray alkali flats in the Great Nevada Desert. From the windows on the left side of the train, they watched with awe as the Humboldt River disappeared into the Great Humboldt Sink, never to emerge. On the right side, they saw the Humboldt Slough (mire), where, less than a decade before, the weary overlanders had to load on their wagons as much of the fetid water that they could carry, in preparation for the dangerous trip across the desert.

Wadsworth, Nevada, was reached at 11:00 P.M. The town was an important rail station with its repair shop, a twenty-stall roundhouse and huge water tank. Engineer S. R. Jenkins took charge at Wadsworth for the next seventy miles.

Humboldt Valley by Thomas Moran. [Central Pacific R. R. Photographic History Museum, Sacramento, CA.]

Meanwhile, more trouble was reported! Word was received of falling boulders up ahead. Ordinarily, such obstructions required the services of an engine with a snow plow mounted in front to clear the road, but to the relief of trainmen and passengers, the boulders proved to be no impediment to traffic.

SUNDAY, JUNE 4

T HE ROWDY TOWN OF RENO, NEVADA (elevation 4,507 feet), lay ahead. Reno began with a population of three people, three pigs and a cow, but the discovery of silver in the region and the coming of the railroad spurred a vigorous growth. Jarrett instructed the engineer to dash through the town without stopping. He gave the fireman some red pyrotechnic powder to sprinkle over the coal and distributed four Roman candles to each passenger. As the Jarrett-Palmer Express rushed through the town, fire belched from the chimney of the engine and hundreds of balls of flame shot out from the windows. Taken unaware, the inhabitants were dazzled by the spectacle and cheered wildly, **293 miles to San Francisco!**

They left Reno at 12:40 A.M. and followed the Truckee River to Truckee (elevation 5,845 feet) on the California border. Finally, they had relief from the monotony of the desert. Immense pine forests surrounded the town and off in the distance rose the majestic crests of the Sierras.

Even before the Central Pacific had completed the track over the Sierra Nevada, it had begun to build eastward from Truckee. The company had managed to transport rolling stock down from the mountains with oxen and wagon and had begun the construction along the trail used by the Forty-Niners, thus qualifying for a generous federal subsidy awarded for each mile of completed track.

Despite the hour (1:56 A.M.), a huge crowd awaited them at Truckee, many of whom held lighted lanterns. Here, a Central

Interior of Snow Shed.
[Central Pacific R. R. Photographic History Museum, Sacramento, CA.]

Donner Lake by Thomas Moran. [Central Pacific R. R. Photographic History Museum, Sacramento, CA.]

Pacific coach with air brakes was cut in behind the engine. *Locomotive #149* was fueled and watered and a helper engine (Barney Kelly, engineer) added to the head end. Engineer Henry Small once again took over the throttle of *#149*.

As the train crossed into California, the passengers prepared themselves for the adventure of a lifetime! Sleep was out of the question! They were about to climb 2,500 feet in fifty miles, then descend 6,000 feet in seventy-five miles, passing through a mile of tunnels. Added to this, the train was determined to establish a new speed record!

It was Theodore D. Judah who had made the early survey of the Sierra Nevadas, choosing the route through the Donner Pass, which had been discovered by a Forty-Niner before the Donner disaster. Sadly, Judah died before the completion of the trans-Sierra track, but the railway remains as a memorial to his remarkable foresight.

As they began the climb with Mt. Rose and Lake Tahoe off to the south, they passed the start of fifty miles of colossal snow sheds. The train climbed the first 1,017 feet in a succession of steep grades, passing Donner Lake. Suddenly they were at Donner Pass, and the passengers shuddered when they recalled the eighty-two emigrants who became snowbound there in 1846 and consumed the flesh of the dead in order to survive. The train sped through two large granite tunnels, one of them the 1,659-foot long Summit Tunnel. The tunnel approaches were supported by a neat rock embankment, called the "China Wall," named for the men who built it. Construction of the Summit Tunnel had consumed a full year of toil, while the railroad investors waited impatiently. Few of the passengers could appreciate the heroic efforts of the twelve thousand Chinese laborers who did the blasting, grading and shoring and the Irish laborers who laid the

Tunnel No. 12.
[Central Pacific R. R. Photographic History Museum, Sacramento, CA.]

track. Near the summit, the road described a switchback of 180 degrees, which ran back on itself at a grade of ninety feet to the mile, all this within fourteen miles of Truckee.

The summit (elevation 7,017 feet) was reached by 2:31 A.M., exactly one hour from Truckee, a record climb. Donner Lake lay to the south, reflected in the ambient light. Other tourists described the scene: "Our first sensation upon its bursting into full view was that of faintness, not from fear but from intense awe." The summit had become a favorite summer resort for Californians. Here, the helper engine was removed and a second coach with air brakes added, to give additional braking power for the descent.

Rounding Cape Horn, California.
[Central Pacific R. R. Photographic History Museum, Sacramento, CA.]

Sunday, June 4

Cisco (elevation 5,939 feet) and Emigrant Gap (elevation 5,221 feet) were quickly passed. At Emigrant Gap a fire engine followed the Jarrett-Palmer Express through the snow sheds as a precaution, since sparks from the engine smokestack could alight the wooden roofs overhead. Six tunnels were traversed on the western side of the summit, the longest measuring 1,800 feet. The train wheels followed the curves along an incredibly narrow ledge excavated from the mountainside. Chinese workmen were said to have worked on the excavation and grading, suspended over the side of the mountains in improvised boatswain's chairs (but some railroad authorities question the story).

The passengers glimpsed the Blue Canyon (elevation 4,677 feet), one thousand feet of sheer precipice below them, with a narrow ribbon of blue water shimmering in the moonlight. But nothing compared with the vista while rounding the incredible Cape Horn, where the railroad clings to the face of a precipice with one thousand feet of cliff above and two thousand feet below. Timid passengers were warned by the guidebooks not to look down. Directly after Cape Horn, American Canyon came into view, with the river winding down through the ravine. The tour book pronounced it "the finest canyon the entire Pacific railway."

American River Cañon.
[Central Pacific R. R. Photographic History Museum, Sacramento, CA.]

By 4:08 A.M. they had descended to Gold Run (elevation 3,206 feet) and the train began to increase speed as it passed the small stations bearing mining town names: "Red Dog," "You Bet," and "Little York." The passengers became frenzied with fear and frantically sought the conductor, but he himself was fully engaged in helping to apply the handbrakes to the Pullman.

As the train rounded a curve off the Long Ravine Trestle, the travelers were suddenly swept off their feet onto the floor of the car. Many screamed. "The velocity with which the train rushed down the incline and the suddenness with which it wheeled around the curves produced a sensation which cannot be reproduced in words," wrote one passenger.

Colfax (elevation 2,421 feet) was reached at 4:30 A.M. and the speed slackened. Onlookers were shouting "Go it!" as the train sped by. It passed Rocklin (elevation 248 feet) in the Sacramento Valley at 5:24 A.M., Roswell at 5:35 A.M. As the sun rose, Sacramento lay off in the distance. Overwhelming excitement gripped the entire train!

Sacramento, California (elevation 30 feet), was a delight to behold at 6:05 in the morning, with its beautiful gardens and palm trees. "The Celestial Flowering Kingdom of the Christian World," proclaimed the guidebooks. Nothing prepared the passengers for the tumultuous reception they were about to receive at the Sacramento station, where a screaming mob surrounded the train and hailed them as conquering heroes.

The two Central Pacific coaches were quickly removed and another added for its air brakes. Coal and water was taken aboard for the final **160 miles to San Francisco.** Since a direct route between Sacramento and Oakland had not yet been constructed, the train was routed to Stockton, doubling the distance. They passed Stockton (elevation 23 feet) without stopping, but took on water at Ellis, where a helper engine was added to the head end for the final grade, since the condition of *#149* was by now a matter of grave concern. The helper remained with them until they reached Altamont at 8:15 A.M., when it was cut out. Off they sped through the Niles Valley to San Leandro. Few had time to read the story of the terrible accident that had occurred here a few years earlier, when an express collided with a local train, because of a tragic switching error. The final two miles along a flat grade were finished in a burst of glory in two minutes flat.

The train arrived at Oakland, California, at 9:20 A.M., and was immediately switched onto the mile-long trestle jutting out onto the bay, said to be the longest trestle in the world. Around the wharf were berthed ocean-going ships and fishing boats flying a host of flags. They blasted their steam whistles as the train appeared. A huge crowd thronged the wharf and watched as eighteen shaken and swaying passengers alighted, all with a four-day growth of beard. With corrections for the difference in longitude, the time between Jersey City and Oakland had been **eighty-three hours, thirty-nine minutes and sixteen seconds** with an average speed of slightly less than forty miles per hour. All this in an age without automatic couplers, heavy rails and well-ballasted tracks, and with inoperative air brakes on the Pullman car two-thirds of the way from Ogden! *Engine #149* had, indeed, made the run from Ogden, but with the aid of two helper engines, three braking coaches and incredible good luck. In all, during the entire journey, the train had stopped seventy-two times and had used twenty engines.

A large steam ferry was at hand to carry the travelers across the bay. As they spied the Golden Gate in the distance, one of the actors surely must have declaimed the oft-quoted words of Horace Greeley:

> Go West, my friends, Go West! Within the Golden Gate lies all that you desire. Go West!

Railroad Ferry Pier, Oakland, California. [Central Pacific R. R. Photographic History Museum, Sacramento, CA.]

Seven minutes later, the party arrived in San Francisco. After adjusting for longitude, latitude and the hocus-pocus factor, the official time was eighty-four hours and seventeen minutes.

A line of hacks was drawn up at the pier awaiting their arrival. The passengers and their baggage were driven in triumph along Market Street, with its wood-planked sidewalks, to the magnificent Palace Hotel, an immense building with seven tiers of bow windows. A cannon atop the hotel boomed out a thirteen-round salute. The whole city seemed to have turned out to greet them.

The Palace Hotel had accommodations for 1,200 guests, corridors two and one half miles long, 437 bath tubs, electric call bells, electric clocks, hydraulic elevators and nine thousand cuspidors. The travelers were driven past iron gates under a stone archway into a regal inner court covered by an immense glass dome. Palm and banana trees lined the circular carriage. Jarrett rushed into the hotel lobby to sign the register at two minutes before 10:00 A.M., followed by the other passengers. The mayor was on hand to great them. Crowds of bystanders pushed their way into the lobby to ogle at the travelers and inspect the hotel register. In the street, bundles of the *Herald* sold for fabulous prices.

A lavish dinner had been prepared in the expectation of a later arrival. Jarrett ordered that the meal be served forthwith to his party and that it be called "breakfast."

The passengers were famished. At long last, they could sit on chairs that did not shake, eat from dishes that did not rattle and drink soup without fear of being scalded. Also in attendance at the historic "breakfast" were the mayor of San Francisco, railroad officials, the press, Army and Navy officers and other dignitaries.

Sunday, June 4

The meal was served on fine Havilland porcelain. Whether the Grand Palace had set out its famous sold gold flatwear is not known. When not in use, the gold utensils were kept across the street in a safe in the Wells-Fargo building.

The breakfast menu consisted of:

> Salmon Grille a la Maitre d'Hotel
> Tom Cod Frit, Sauce Tartare
> Cucumber Salad
> Filet de Boef, Sauce Bearnaise
> Cotelettes d'Agneau, Sauce Soubise
> Escalope de Veau a la Guennoise
> Pomme de Terre, Maitre d'Hotel
> Rognon Saute au Champignons
> Poulet Grille a la Cresson
> Oeufs Brouilles au Point d'Asperges
> Oeufs Frits en Temben
> Pre-Sale
> > Apricots, Raspberries, Strawberries, Cherries

After the speeches and toasts, the actors retired to their rooms to prepare for their appearance on stage at the McCullough Theater the following day (Monday, June 5). They shaved off their scruffy beards and spread themselves out on their luxurious beds. Lawrence Barrett later remarked that he had difficulty falling asleep until the bellhop shook the bed and threw handsful of cinders on his face.

Henry V proved to be an enormous success, if not a sensation. For the rest of their run, the actors played to a full house and enthusiastic audiences. Wrote one dissenting newsman: "The crowd is intent in making heroes of those foolhardy men who took their lives into their hands to gain notoriety."

Many newspapers hailed the trip in editorials. Most prescient of all were the remarks of the *New York Herald*:

> Perhaps the most remarkable thing about the journey is that it has not required any other appliance to complete it than those already in use, except the injection of that quality which today we call enterprise.

After a week, the party dispersed and all too quickly the limelight dimmed on the historic trip.

The record of eighty-three hours, thirty-nine minutes remained unbroken until 1906, when, following the San Francisco earthquake, E. H. Harriman ran a special train that made the run to New York in seventy-one hours and twenty-seven minutes. This record stood until 1934 when the Union Pacific ran a streamliner from Los Angeles to New York in fifty-six hours and fifty-five minutes.

The careers of Jarrett and Palmer were short lived. In 1877, they brought *Uncle Tom's Cabin* to Great Britain. Palmer died in London in July of the following year. Jarrett settled in Britain and lived there for two decades as his fame slowly faded. He died of heart failure in London on October 14, 1903. A week later, there was a brief mention of his passing in the *New York Daily Graphic*. James Gordon Bennett left the United States and moved to France. He settled in Paris and Beaulieu, and directed the operations of the *Herald* from abroad.

The American rail system continued to grow during the first half of the twentieth century, but, thereafter, for a multitude of reasons, it was allowed to decline, overtaken by the great railroads of Europe and Asia. Today, the American rail system slumbers, like the fairy princess in the storybook, awaiting the reviving kiss of a Prince Charming.

BIBLIOGRAPHY

Secondary Sources

Beebe, Lucius. *Mansions on Wheels.* Berkeley, California: Howell-North, 1959.

Bowles, Samuel. *The Pacific Railroad Open.* Boston: Fields, Osgood, 1869.

http://www.cprr.org/Museum/Bowles_1869.html

Brown, Dee Alexander. *The Year of the Century: 1876.* New York: Scribner, 1966.

Carter, Charles Frederick. *When Railroads Were New.* New York: Holt, 1910.

Conkey, Kelli. *Leg Drama.* University of California at Irvine, student paper.

http://www.humanities.uci.edu/litjourn/students/writing/conkeylegdrama.pdf

Coolidge, Susan [aka Sarah Chauncey Woolsey]. "A Few Hints on the California Journey," *Scribner's Monthly*, May, 1873.

Douglas, George H. *All Aboard!* New York: Paragon, 1992.

Creagan, Leo F. "The Steam of '76," *Union Pacific Magazine*, March, 1923, p. 6.

Grant, Mark. *The Rise and Fall of the Broadway Musical.* Boston: Northeastern Press, 2004.

Crofutt, George A. *Crofutt'sTrans-Continental Tourist Guide.* New York: American News Co., 1869.

Gilliss, John R. "Tunnels of the Pacific Railroad," in Van Nostrand's *Eclectic Engineering Magazine*, Vol. II, 1970.

http://cprr.org/Museum/Tunnels.html

Joslyn, D. "The Jarrett and Palmer Special 1876," (Talk given to the Railway and Locomotive Historical Society, Oakland WHARF meeting Room, June 1933). Published in *Bulletin* No 11, RLHS, 1926.

Joslyn, D. L. and J. O. Goodell. "The Jarrett and Palmer Special" (typed notes: courtesy of the California State Railroad Museum Library).

Kalmbach, Al H., Linn H. Westcott, Willard V. Anderson (eds.). "The Jarrett-Palmer Express." *Trains*, Vol. 3, December 1942, p. 10.

Nordhoff, Charles. "California," *Harper's New Monthly Magazine*, New York: Harper & Bros., May, 1872

http://www.cprr.org/Museum/Nordhoff.html

O'Connor, Richard. *The Scandalous Mr. Bennett.* Garden City, New York: Doubleday, 1962.

Leslie, Mrs. Frank. *California: A Pleasure Trip from Gotham to the Golden Gate.* New York: Carleton, 1877.

Nelsons' Pictorial Guide-books. *The Central Pacific Railroad: A Trip across the North American Continent from Ogden to San Francisco.* New York: T. Nelson and Sons, 1871.

Odom, L. G. "The Black Crook at Niblo's Garden," *The Drama Review*, Vol. 26, Spring, 1882.

Owens, Richard Henry. *Peaceful Warrior, A Biography of Horace Porter,* New York: Garland Publishing, 1990.

Robinson, N. "The Comforts and Discomforts of Travel," *Frank Leslie's Popular Monthly*, August, 1882.

Root, Henry. *Personal History and Reminiscences.* San Francisco: Private Circulation, 1921 [Central Pacific Railroad Photographic History Museum] http://cprr.org/Museum/Henry_Root_1921.html

Sante, Luc. *Low Life.* New York: Ferrar-Straus-Giroux, 1991.

Bibliography

Stevenson, Robert Louis. *Across the Plains.* London: Chattus & Windus, 1892.

Stewart, E.S. "Whirled across the Continent," *Trains*, Vol. 15, No 6, p. 27.

Strobridge, Edson T. *The Central Pacific Railroad and the Legend of Cape Horn, 1865-1866.* San Luis Obispo, CA: privately printed, 2001. http://cprr.org/Museum/Cape_Horn.html

Taylor, Benjamin. *Between the Gates.* Chicago: S.C. Griggs and Company, 1878.

http://cprr.org/Museum/Between_the_Gates/index.html

Whitton, J. *The Naked Truth.* Philadelphia: Shaw, 1897.

Williams, Henry T. *The Pacific Tourist.* New York: Williams, 1877.

Wilmeth, Don. *Cambridge Guide to American Theatre.* Cambridge: Cambridge University Press, 1993.

Newspapers

Newark Daily Advertiser, June 1 to 4, 1876

New York Herald, June 1 to 6, 1876.

Daily Cincinnati Gazette, June 2, 3, and 5, 1876.

Frank Leslie's Illustrated Newspaper, February 9, 1878, p. 385.

INDEX

Allegheny Mountains, ascent, 29
Allen, William, engineer, 49
Altoona, Pennsylvania, famous horseshoe curve, 18
American River Canyon, 71
Arndt, Dr. A., passenger, 14
Arrival ceremonies, 77
Arrival in San Francisco, 76
Astor Hotel, 16
"Baggage smashers", 21
Baltimore & Ohio Railroad, 29
Baltimore Sun, newspaper, 29
Barras, Charles M., author of *The Black Crook*, 3
Barrett, Lawrence, star of *Henry V*, 8, 16, 28, 46, 77
Bennett, James Gordon Jr, publisher of *New York Herald*, 5, 7, 11, 15, 78
Bishop, C. P., 16
Blue Canyon, 71
Booth, Edwin, 8
Booth, Junius Brutus, 2
Booth Theater, 8
Boynsenn, John, engineer, 37
Braking systems, 18, 19, 50, 58, 60, 72
Cape Horn, 71
Caril, Henry, passenger, 14
Centennial Exposition, 1

Central Pacific Railroad, 9, 12, 52, 55, 56, 58, 59, 65, 73
    gave money and free passes to Indian Chiefs, 45
Chambers, Andrew, engineer, 28
Charleston-Hamburg Railroad, 8
Cheyenne, Wyoming, 46
Chicago and North Western Railroad, 34, 37, 56
Chicago Express, 32
Chimney Rock, Nebraska, 44
Chinese laborers, 52–54, 58, 68, 71
Civil War, 9
Cody, Buffalo Bill, 7
Columbus, Nebraska, 42
"Combine", 22
Commissary Car, #202, 20, 22
Conductor, 27
Continental Divide, 47, 49
Cowboys, 45
Crash of 1857, 39
Creamer, Thomas J., passenger, 14
Crocker, Charles, financier, 56
Dale River Bridge, 47
Departure festivities, 16, 27
Devil's Gap, 55

Devil's Slide, 53
Dickens, Charles, 7
Dodge, Grenville, surveyor, 47
Dom Pedro II, Emperor of Brazil, 1
Donner Lake, 69
Donner Pass, 68
Dougherty, T., passenger, 14
Dressing and toilet area ("saloon"), 25
Echo Canyon, 53
Echo Valley, 54
Eldridge, F.W., passenger, 14
Emerson, Warren, passenger, 14
Emigrant trains, 39
Engine
 #146, 39
 #149, Black Fox, 56, 60, 68, 73, 74
 #151, 50
 #153, 52
 #156, 43
 #167, 49
 #168, 46
 #169, 51
 #199, 32
 #221, 33
 #26, 31
 #77, 44
 American Class D type 4-4-0, 20
 Charles Dow, 37
 Governor Tilden #573, 20, 21, 29
 Hookset, 37
 L. Holbrook, 37
 W. A. Booth, 37

Erie Canal, 2
Evans, Oliver, 8
Evanston Age, newspaper, 52
Express route
 Altoona, Pennsylvania, 29
 Battle Mountain, Nevada, 60
 Bitter Creek, Wyoming, 51
 Bridger, Wyoming, 51
 Carlin, Nevada, 60
 Cheyenne, Wyoming, 46
 Chicago, 34
 Cisco, California, 71
 Council Bluffs, Iowa, 38
 Donner Pass, 68
 Elko, Nevada, 59, 60
 Emigrant Gap, 71
 Evanston, Wyoming, 52
 Fort Wayne, 30
 Fulton, Illinois, 37
 Gold Run, California, 72
 Grand Island, Nebraska, 42
 Green River Station, Wyoming, 51
 Harrisburg, 28
 Humboldt River, 60
 Jersey City, 17
 Kelton, Utah, 58
 Lake Tahoe, 68
 Laramie City, 49
 Medicine Bow, Wyoming, 49
 Mississippi River, 35
 North Platte, Nebraska, 44
 Oakland, California, 74
 Ogden, Utah, 55
 Omaha, 38
 Philadelphia, 28
 Pittsburgh, 30

Index

Express route (cont.)
Promontory, Utah, 58
Reno, Nevada, 65
Sacramento, California, 73
San Francisco, California, 76
San Leandro, California, 73
Sherman Summit, 47
Sidney, Nebraska, 45
Stockton, California, 73
Toano, Nevada, 59
Truckee, California, 68
Wadsworth, Nevada, 61
Wells, Nevada, 59
Winnemucca, Nevada, 61
Falling boulders, 63
Farewell dinner, theater tradition, 16
Forest, Edward, 2
Forty-Niners, 65
Grand Island, Nebraska, 42
Grand Palace Hotel, San Francisco, 13, 76
 breakfast menu, 77
"Great American Desert", 41, 51, 59
Great Humboldt Sink, 61
Great Salt Lake, 58
Great Salt Lake Valley, 55
Greeley, Horace, 74
Guidebooks, 27
Harriman, E.H., broke record in 1906, 78
Haupt, Herman, 12, 14
Henry V
 final performance in New York, 16
 to run in San Francisco, 8
 in San Francisco, 77

"High ball", 31
"Hobo", 47
Hoffmaster, Sol, engineer, 29
Hopkins, Mark, financier, 56
Horseshoe Bend, 29
"Hot boxes", 50, 57, 59
"Hot shot", 31
Hotel Car, *Thomas A. Scott*, 20
Humboldt River, 60, 61
Humboldt Slough, 61
Huntington, Collis P., financier, 56
Hutchins, Frank, engineer, 51
Independence Rock, 52
Indians, at the Sidney train station, 45
Irish laborers, 58
Jackson, John, engineer, 37
Jarrett, Henry C., 3, 7, 15, 16, 27, 28, 46, 51, 52, 65
 devises plan for cross-country express, 8, 10–12
 short career, 78
 theater producer, 2
Jenkins, S.R., engineer, 61
Jersey City, 74
Journal box, 50, 61
Judah, Theodore D., 68
 surveyor-engineer, 56
Keefe, Thomas, engineer, 37
Kelker, A., engineer, 32
Kelly, Barney, engineer, 68
Kerr, David, engineer, 21
La Biche au Bois, integrated with *The Black Crook*, 2
Lake Tahoe, 68
Laramie City, 49
Lewis and Clark, 38

Lloyd, W., engineer, 43
Long Ravine Trestle, 73
Menu, typical, 24
Miller, Robert, engineer, 50
Mohawk and Hudson railroad line, 8
Monere, Alfred, passenger, 14
Mormon laborers, 54
Mormons, 55
Morrison, Alfred, passenger, 14
Morrison, Hyatt, passenger, 14
New York Central Railroad, 18, 29
New York City, theaters, 2
New York Herald, 33, 39, 52, 60, 76, 78
   newspapers carried on board, 22, 28, 30, 34, 56
Niblo Gardens, theater, 3, 7
North Platte, Nebraska, 44
Oakland, California, 74
Ogden, Utah, 55
Pacific Central Railroad, 12
Pacific Express, 42
Paiute Indians, 61
Palmer, Henry (Harry), 3, 7, 15, 16, 30
   short career, 78
   theater producer, 2
Panama Railroad, 9
Parker, E.N., passenger, 14
Passengers, aboard the express, 14
Pennsylvania Central Railroad, 30
Pennsylvania Railroad, 12, 16–18, 27, 29

Philadelphia
   Centenary grounds, 28
   train station, 28
Philips, William, engineer, 29
Pickering, Philip, engineer, 37
Pierce, Carl, engineer, 44
Pittsburgh, Forth Wayne and Chicago Railroad, 31
Platte River, 41, 42
Polliemus, A.H., engineer, 33
Pony Express, 45
Porter, Horace, 34
   vice president of Pullman Company, 11, 12
Powell, John Wesley, 51
Power, Tyrone, 2
Prairie dog villages, 45
Preston, Augustus H., engineer, 34
Prior, Milton, passenger, 14
Promontory Point, Utah, 9, 54, 55
Promontory, Utah, 58
Pullman, George, 11, 12
Pullman Hotel Cars, 25
Pullman Palace Hotel Car, 20, 56
   Marlborough #311, 20, 22
Railroads, early history in America, 8–10
Rawlins, John, 50
Rawson, P., passenger, 14
Reno, Nevada, 65
Reynolds, Doc, engineer, 52
Rice, engineer, 61
Risks of train travel, 19
Rocky Mountains, 46
Russell, "Bull Run", passenger, 14

Index

Sacramento, California, 73
"Saloon", 25
San Francisco, California, 76
Scott, Thomas A., 14, 18
   president of Pennsylvania Railroad, 12
Seating areas, 24, 25
Sherman Summit, the world's highest railraod track, 47
"Shoo fly", 53, 54
Sidney, Nebraska, 45
Sierra Nevada Mountains, 56, 65
Silverstine, Meyer, passenger, 14
Sleeping areas, 24
Sleeping car, *Yosemite*, 20
Small, Henry, 68
   engineer, 56, 57
Smith, Benjamin, Chief Engineer, 57, 59
Snow sheds, 49
Speed, 15, 73
Stanford, Leland, financier, 56
Stevens, John, 8
Stevenson, Robert Louis, 33
Suez Canal, 9
Summit Tunnel, 68
Tabor, G., engineer, 31
Temple, Charles, 2
Temple, Fanny, 2
"Ten Mile Track", 58
The Black Crook, 3
   extravagant stage set, 3
   most successful production on Broadway, 5
   plot, 2, 3
   revived in vaudeville and silent film, 7

Thorpe, Fred, 16
"Thousand Mile Tree", 53, 54
Tickets, made especially for the occasion, 13
Track pans (water troughs), 18
Tramps, 46, 47
Transcontinental railroad, 9
Travel, transcontinental, 10
Truckee, California, 65
Twain, Mark, 7
Uncle Tom's Cabin, 78
Union Pacific Railroad, 9, 10, 14, 38, 41, 49, 50, 52, 54–56, 58, 78
   Indian troubles, 45
United New Jersey Railroad and Canal Company, 17
Vanderbilt, Cornelius, 18
Vanwormers, John, engineer, 32
Wagner Hotel Cars, 25
Waiters and attendants, 24
Wasatch Mountains, 53
Wash-out, 53
Weber Canyon, 53
Weber River, 54
Weeks, Nicholas, engineer, 46
Weid, C.A., passenger, 14
Westinghouse braking system, 18, 19
Whitman, Walt, 7
Williams, C.F., 32, 39
   passenger, 14
Wilson, Woodrow, 7
Wood, E.B., engineer, 39
Wright, James, engineer, 56, 57
Young, Brigham, 54, 55, 57

About the Author

Dr. J. C. Ladenheim is a retired neurosurgeon and student of nineteenth-century American history. His recent books, *Alien Horseman* and *Custer's Thorn*, both published by Heritage Books, deal with the Custer saga. His forthcoming *Abe Lincoln Afloat* describes Lincoln's oft-neglected trips to New Orleans.

www.ingramcontent.com/pod-product-compliance
Lightning Source LLC
Chambersburg PA
CBHW070311100426
42743CB00011B/2439